Horses Where the Answers
Should Have Been

D1051376

BOOKS BY CHASE TWICHELL

Horses Where the Answers Should Have Been

Dog Language

The Lover of God (translations of Rabindranath Tagore,
with Tony K. Stewart)

The Snow Watcher

The Ghost of Eden

The Practice of Poetry: Writing Exercises from Poets Who Teach
(co-edited with Robin Behn)

Perdido

The Odds

Northern Spy

CHASE TWICHELL

Horses Where the Answers Should Have Been

New and Selected Poems

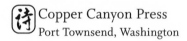
Copper Canyon Press
Port Townsend, Washington

Cover art: Grant Hayunga, *Pronghorn Boy*, 2004. Mixed media, 50 × 50 inches.

"Skeleton": The Bob Dylan lines are from *Don't Look Back,* D.A. Pennebaker's documentary film of Dylan's 1965 tour of England.

"Dangerous Playgrounds": The quoted passage is misremembered from "The Mystic" by Cale Young Rice (*The Little Book of Modern Verse,* Houghton Mifflin, 1913). The poem also paraphrases parts of *The Tale of Two Bad Mice* by Beatrix Potter (F. Warne, 1904).

"Cities of Mind": The James Richardson quote is from *Vectors: Aphorisms and Ten-Second Essays* (Ausable Press, 2001).

Copper Canyon Press is in residence at Fort Worden State Park in Port Townsend, Washington, under the auspices of Centrum. Centrum is a gathering place for artists and creative thinkers from around the world, students of all ages and backgrounds, and audiences seeking extraordinary cultural enrichment.

LIBRARY OF CONGRESS CATALOGING-IN-PUBLICATION DATA

Twichell, Chase, 1950–
Horses where the answers should have been: new and selected poems / Chase Twichell.
    p. cm.
Includes bibliographical references.
ISBN 978-1-55659-318-5 (pbk.: alk. paper)
1. Title.
PS3570.W47H67 2010
811'.54 —dc22

2009048885

9 8 7 6 5 4 3 2 FIRST PRINTING

COPPER CANYON PRESS
Post Office Box 271
Port Townsend, Washington 98368

www.coppercanyonpress.org

for Ann Chase Twichell Hendrie

ACKNOWLEDGMENTS

Sincere thanks to the editors of the following magazines, where some of these poems were first published.

AGNI Online: "Tenderfoot"

Alaska Quarterly Review: "Savin Rock"

Alhambra Poetry Calendar 2008 (Belgium): "Tourist Traps"

Field: "Cold Water"

Gulf Coast: "Playgrounds of Being"

Hamilton Stone Review: "Mask of a Maiden," "The Fifth Precept," "Zazen and Opium"

The Kenyon Review: "The Long Bony Faces of the Mules," "My Lethe"

The Laurel Review: "Snakeskin"

The Massachusetts Review: "Sayonara Marijuana Mon Amour"

New England Review: "Math Trauma," "The Dark Rides"

The New Republic: "Snow-globe of Vesuvius," "Negligent Worldicide"

Poetry London (U.K.): "Snow-globe of Vesuvius," "The Long Bony Faces of the Mules," "Tomboyhood," "Savin Rock," "My Lethe"

Salamander: part of "Good-bad Zazen" (as "Dogen's Question"), "The Fork"

Salmagundi: "How Zen Ruins Poets"

Scarab (online): "Tomboyhood"

Smartish Pace: "From a Distance"

Tricycle: "Old-lady Cautious on the Stairs"

West Branch: "Walky-talky," "Clouds and Water"

The Yale Review: "Sideshows," "Forensic Interludes," "War Porn"

RB, my beloved—twenty-three years; so far so good.

Deep gratitude to:

Dr. Neil Horowitz at Dana-Farber Cancer Institute, for saving my life.

John Daido Loori Roshi, Geoffrey Shugen Arnold, Konrad Ryushin Marchaj, Jody Hojin Kimmel, and all the monastics at Zen Mountain Monastery, for their teachings.

Seido Ray Ronci at Hokoku-an Zendo for his friendship and example.

Eliza Twichell. Words do not suffice.

Contents

from *Perdido*   1991

from *The Ghost of Eden*   1995

from *The Snow Watcher*   1998

from *Dog Language*   2005

*Horses Where the Answers
Should Have Been*   New Poems

Horses Where the Answers
Should Have Been

from

Northern Spy

1981

Inland

Above the blond prairies,
the sky is all color and water.
The future moves
from one part to another.

This is a note
in a tender sequence
that I call love,
trying to include you,
but it is not love.
It is music, or time.

To explain the pleasure I take
in loneliness, I speak of privacy,
but privacy is the house around it.
You could look inside,
as through a neighbor's window
at night, not as a spy
but curious and friendly.
You might think
it was a still life you saw.

Somewhere, the ocean
crashes back and forth
like so much broken glass,
but nothing breaks.
Against itself,
it is quite powerless.

Irises have rooted
all along the fence,
and the barbed berry-vines
gone haywire.

Unpruned and broken,
the abandoned orchard
reverts to the smaller,
harder fruits, wormy and tart.
In the stippled shade,
the fallen pears move
with the soft bodies of wasps,
and cows breathe in
the licorice silage.

It is silent
where the future is.
No longer needed there,
love is folded away in a drawer
like something newly washed.
In the window,
the color of the pears intensifies,
and the fern's sporadic dust
darkens the keys of the piano.

Clouds containing light
spill out my sadness.
They have no sadness of their own.

The timeless trash of the sea
means nothing to me—

its roaring descant,
its multiple concussions.
I love painting more than poetry.

A Mysterious Heart

I don't like what the world has become.
At night, the sprinklers sound like rain
but I am neither fooled nor consoled.

Real rain no longer exists,
and the fish in the rivers
flash with phosphorus.

In secret I compile the history
of the world before the tragedy,
a lonely occupation. As a foreigner,

I write in a language of immunity,
make notes of things, deciphering,
invisible as a tourist.

Inside the nebulous skies,
millions of tiny planes
disperse their seed,

and the radio calls it weather.
There was weather in my childhood
on the other planet,

not that it was lovely. It was cold.
It was lovely, but cold.
When, in my investigations,

I search through the scrapbooks
for proof of this,
I discover the pictures, six to a page,

entangled in a white trellis,
the space around them.
This is the way I remember

Father's house, a square of darkness
crisscrossed by the moon,
a latticework the ivy climbed.

That's me in the window,
wondering about love.
I had a mysterious heart.

Perhaps my present disorientation
began on such a night.
In the many layers of the sky,

the stars appeared to swim
and multiply, like snow, or sperm,
or the white cells of death

on the laboratory slide.
Or maybe it was Christmas,
and other people had the Spirit,

but I never had it, as far as I know.
But all childhoods are hazardous,
and their cruelties ordinary.

I love the snowfall,
the blossoms of silence
that gather around us.

Then this planet is cast as the other,
and my life as another's.
The planes dive toward terra firma

with ice on their wings, which is justice,
their cockpits full of moonlight.
So whether the water spills

through the pipes and spigots
or freezes in the heavens,
it makes no difference.

I come from the snowbound planet,
so far away it seems a spark,
a chip of ice. The truth is,

I did not consent to exile here.
So the mind goes into the past,
or up into a clean, new galaxy.

Northern Lights

I soak the clothes,
cold water a relief,
and slump in the hammock

peeling an orange, throwing the peels
into the coiled green garden hose.
The lights start up again.

We don't need them.
A plump bird spits in the oven,
dripping fat. Upstairs,

you're typing again: work noise,
the slow fan, a fine sweat
on your skin. I yell, *Want anything?*

but you don't hear. From the road,
the smell of gasoline.
No one told us it was alarming,

this attrition,
this chafing of cold, unironed sheets,
or that the sky whips itself for us:

clean pink welts, the sting of infection.
It steeps our house in its ray-light:
the woman fixed in her hammock,

the man who pretends to himself
he comforts her,
who does comfort her.

This Was a Farm

This was a farm. A tractor
without tires rusts in the yard.
Did we come, clothes full of burrs,
to be saddened by the house,
its roof buckled, collapsing?

Or to listen for ourselves
in the whine of the coiled wire?
Whole panes unbroken. The world
flowers in the inward pink
convolutions of the sky;

hay without color thrashes
around us, and no cattle
drink at the metal basins.
We could become this, complete
as the barn door opening,

banging, opening, banging.
All we have to do is stay.
Live here. Give up everything.
Never speak, or sleep. Even
now, the memory flinches

within us, and we long for
a home in the cold, stopped light,
the salt licks, the barn. See how
the roof takes fire, kindling the
sun and corrugated tin.

Reno

Women love emotions.
One by one we appear
in the palace of machinery and lights
as though fresh from spa waters,
and stroll through the tourists
enthralled by the elegant flow
of money out of their lives.
They are underdressed for the desert
this time of year.
In the glittering aisles,
the stars and cherries
whirl on their spools
and do not align.
Parts of heaven must be
that mathematical,
since some minds are uncomfortable
off in the billows,
where it is too soft.
I am not distracted by emotion.
I use it. A cold man is an inspiration.
So I appear excitable, unhinged,
and sit at a table of perfect green,
and win. Love is a country
to which we return and return,
but in which we cannot live.

Snow Light

I stop, winded, the air sifting down.
Here is the peculiar light I hoped for.
The branches of the pines are lobed with snow,
each shape intact, and brightened from within.

I walked among these flickering trunks in fall,
the grass grown stiff and noisy underfoot,
and found a mystery, a tree, a flowering quince,
all pale and fragrant, out of season.

It gave off this light.
What is holy is earth's unearthliness.
Love, could we describe it,
would break apart, lucency and force.

A starling rasps from his white precinct.
Far back in the woods, the snow is falling again,
perhaps into your life. The wind returns
to chisel its drifts and ribbing.

Forgive the rounded burdens of the branches.
They do not suffer, suffused in this light.
They are not sorrows,
though that is the meaning we give them.

The Iris, That Sexual Flower

The iris, that sexual flower,
holds itself closed.
The florist's bucket is blue
with closed flowers:
bunches of irises
wet with their sap
printing the eyes.
The tongue in the mouth
knows the blueprint,
the promise: the tongue on the neck.

The stems in the pail swim downward,
pulling up water. Water's the weight
of the swimmer, the eyelids,
the cords of the neck,
the collarbone, wishbone,
the speaking power of the mouth.
A kiss gives the mouth a drink.
Give me a drink.
The blue iris opens in the heart,
that bucket, in sexual water.

Your Eightieth

There is death in old postcards,
death in the sack of trash.
The future of the house is overgrown.
You mention it, the briars at the screens.
The sky reminds you of the sky
in your childhood, before thunder.
Even then, the white pines shook
and darkened, as though great birds
had come to roost in them.
The west wind opens, and water
streams out into the world,
though to hear you tell it,
we're in for a drought.
More fires, and the river is lower.
Your shawl has slipped from your bones again.
The arms wave me away.
You make a fragile music
with the ice in your glass.
Bourbon is your next-to-last reward.
The rugged flapping in the thick boughs
could be the wind come to fetch you,
or angels with a family likeness,
their powerful, averted faces
stiff with human love for you.

The Dim Parade

The dogs have dragged a deer's head
into the yard. The neck bone points
to the raw east, where the sun
pries light from a cloud.
Summer, the bitter black lips.

To escape this we drive all day
through towns that disturb us,
their windows full of dust.
Who whistles in the woods?
We begin to pass houses that fascinate.

Some sadness is inherited. Not all sadness.
These houses have a certain look,
as though the lives inside them
were stenciled, one over another.
Even the barns that redden in the rain
hold nothing but lives halfway to the boneyard,
horses and cattle and those that feed them.
And so we drive, to pass the dim parade.

Some pain is instructive. Not all pain.
Next to the blackening gardens
and rooms that darken,
heaven is a white place.
A matted cow, showing her ribs,
turns her single, delicate horn toward us.
She stands in withered grass,

in a field bathed by storm-light.
Such frail tinder.
Warfare makes that black and white debris.

In the town of white stones,
a tractor cuts the tall grass
soundlessly, and the rain soaks down
into the cold compartments, the honeycomb.
Mown grass is the scent of the dead.

Like a Caretaker

I live here, but do not live here.
Trash blows through the sky tonight.
Out of a snowy tree, the stars appear,

drops of ice water, they seem so pure.
The tree petrifies. They are its parasites.
I live here, but do not live here.

Fusion was the word I loved—its nuclear
logic. The world with a heart of dynamite.
Out of a snowy tree, the stars appear

faceted and cold, an elegant prayer
addressed to Death. Death loves black and white.
I live here, but do not live here.

Creatures are born from atoms, from air,
parentless, and drift like satellites
out of a snowy tree. The stars appear

to be parts of a machine in disrepair,
which I do not repair. And for this oversight,
I live here, but do not live here.
Out of a snowy tree, the stars appear.

Nostalgia for the Future

A cold joy leaps from the orchard
in early evening,
when the pear and apple flower.
Their petals enclose
the nubs of the unformed fruits
with a private dampness.
Cattle drift through the fields
like headstones, and soon
the sky will spill its milky light
down almost into the trees.

Children are swimming
in a limestone pool
under other trees.
Clouded and still, the water
passes from white to dark
without a trace of blueness.
Each pale body liquefies.

A man winds his watch
in the merciful near-dark.
He lies on a mound of soft grasses,
this year's and last year's,
in the orchard of scent and wetness.
His children have slept
past their births.
They swim in the trees
among lime-pale flowers.

His story is sad and ordinary.
The ghosts in the leaves
are telling it again:
the beautiful towns of childhood,
the marriages and deaths.
Disconsolate, they are always
coming and going away,
fluttering the limpid pear flowers.
Disturbed by the color
of clouds at night,
and stung by the minor lights
of the fireflies,
they whisper their longing.
Unkissed, their mouths are hard
and tender as the final pear.

Watercress and Ice

The grass gave way, and suddenly
you were thigh-deep in water so cold
it made you forget yourself.
You saw two great blue herons,
and mention these things in your letter.
The brilliant, green-white substance
you walked through was watercress,
watercress and ice. I can see you,
underdressed, wading out
into the breakable, ice-invaded plants.

I cut these lilacs from the wet hedge
half-bloomed, cold to the touch.
Their fragrance has none of the
delicious bitterness you walk through.
The transient herons have gone,
taking their blue lives home.
It's a northerner's story to be cold,
though you know we unfold our maps
with explicit tenderness.
And the lilacs are bitterly beautiful,
opening already in the warm room,
purple and simple,
because I make you see them.
We will not find the wilderness
where we expect it,
nor find, in cold, a home.

The Billowing Lights

Someone appears
in the trackless, floating field,
a body the color of cloud,
or the gauze that's
slowly stripped away
after sleep or sex,
or genuine pain.
It is a soul
who cautiously looks down,
deciding to stay
in the changeable vapors,
small and unborn,
abstract as a crystal,
and have that be its life.

Where they are,
they are safe from fire
and the transforming cold,
safe from money.
And yet,
in certain kinds of weather,
they draw near
as if for comfort,
as people are drawn
to a snowy, foreign place
after marriage or a loss.
They press into the leaves
of trees made explicit by rain,

there in the radiant dark
like a black migration.
Or quite overtly
in a day of blindness,
they come close
to ask for something,
but all we hear
is the dry snow,
its whispering friction,
and the scraping
engines of the plows.

Perhaps it is the sexual
dream they long for,
the ways we have
of thwarting the filthy rains,
and blood and age.
They may come down
out of the sorrowful air,
lured by the billowing
lights of wars
like fish to inedible glitter,
that longing the one
force of their lives.

They peer down
into the earthly light,
the delicate towns
burning in the radium
of the future,
and the white air falling.
Little fossil ghosts,

they grow dim and quiet,
embedded in the sky.
And tonight, to keep them
from the slicing wind,
I do not want them.

His Shoulders in the Water

He swims into the reflections of clouds,
the purple, plantless depth
of the space between them.
The specific poisons of insects
have raised a dozen welts on his back,
which he soothes in the cold anesthetic
of a lake without boat or dock.
In early spring the windows of the cottages
fill with the sky's white musculature.
Shadowy lilacs move around them,
gray-blue, uncorrupted by children.
No rough towels dry on the grass.
His shoulders shudder in the water,
embracing and letting go,
striped by the ladders of cold
down which he could climb
into the intimate currents
where the dead swim, half-awake
and slippery with memory.
All around him they rise
to feed on the particles
of light his pale feet leave,
thrashing in the part of the sky
that is moving away
and yet always here.

from

The Odds

1986

Meteor Showers, August 1968

A night in August,
in my adolescence,
perseveres intact.
An isolated night,
muscular with cold,
pinned open to reveal
a darkened gulf
filled with the talc
of disembodied minerals.

Part of the mind still lies
on a splintery wooden bench,
hostage to the sparks
that brightened
at their moment of extinction.
Austere, remembered acres…
embers turning inward
to blue-blackness.

Meteors raked the atmosphere,
each one a struck match,
a cat's scratch of light.

Words also fall
across enormous blackness,
small spilled baskets.
Abandoned in that wilderness,
they turn toward one another

and marry, midsentence,
becoming in effect
a paradigm of the mind's decorum,
the balance it requires
to hold its illusion of stillness.
It seems that the mind
must renounce
the form that contains it
to swim in the deep,
directionless waters,
or that it must stand
as a stockade or a dam,
opposed to the
starry, immortal flood.

Cedar Needles

Vendors croon their welcoming harangues
as we pass pyramids of duck eggs,
cheap dresses, black cheeses,
and the shrunken
mummies of the smoked quail,

but we follow the scent of cedar
up into a valley
of sheep and wind-toughened flowers,
the needles
slippery beneath our feet.

Goats scatter uneasily away,
dung rank in their crusted hides.

The rooftops disappear below us,
hazed by the violet smut of cooking.
Here and there the sun
points out a metal gutter.
The clay tiles shiver in the heat.

At this height,
cow bells and church bells
belong to the wild music of the place.
We are farther from God than ever,
at home among the uncountable,
the yellow denial of their split-eyes.

Blighted with plastic flowers,
the homely little cemeteries
embedded in the hillsides
become another landscape
arrested by the camera,
as one tourist
fixes the other there forever.
Strange to think
we have climbed this far
for only another view of ourselves,
the world being
everywhere equally foreign.

Planet of Smoke and Cloud

The earth could not keep
its dead in storage.
Cirrus, stratus, the sky
sloughed off their cloudy migrations.
Tides of wars spilled back and forth
across the phantom boundaries
in the naturalization of dust to dust,
dust the pale colors of human countries.
In a brilliancy of particles
the atoms combined and recombined,
flashing in the grim kinetics
of the earth dispersed
back into its elements,
and with it everything else:
hydrogen, the rippling fires,
our numberless obsessions
with love and power,
all bathed in the spiritual
phosphorus of the afterglow.
Of all the worlds lost
in the hopeless ascension
of matter toward God,
one was a fluke of aesthetics.
A hand's rayed bones
could be a bird's wing,
inscrutable fossil
locked in a radiant cinder.

Evening, Herron's Farm

Lit by kerosene,
the windows of the milking barn
recall the dearly departed light.

The basket of early apples
will be heavy by nightfall,
empty again by dawn.

Aligned in the cool apparatus,
the black-and-white bodies shift
and lean, their hooves and udders
shell and ivory
in a realm of little color.
Milk spurts
into the glass globes overhead.

In the old graveyard
the stones have long since
tipped into the lengthening grass.

The animals bide in dusky quarters,
drowsing over the coarse
molasses of fodder.

I can almost penetrate
their remote intelligence,
bedding down in twilight
under the broken music.

Watercress trembles in the brook,
bitter as the wish to come home
to this place,
where all my sufferings
would be imaginable.

Japanese Weeping Cherry

The bed seems a raft set adrift
in the inadequate moonlight
by which I write.
The weeping cherry
drowns in its blanching waters,
trailing shell-pink sprays
across the screens.

Time is a foreignness
in the forms of things.
Asymmetrical and Japanese,
a tree enters a poem
and is fixed there,
an ignorant stroke of blossoms.
Anything can be corrupted
for the sake of a new pureness.

How easily one form
infects another:
moonlight falters in the leaves,
love holds it there.
The tree becomes
corsages crumbling in a drawer.
And there is never an end to this,
except when consciousness ends,
and it does not end here.

The Hotel du Nord

On the lawn of the old hotel at twilight
a boy stands swathed in a white towel,
his hair still damp from the lake.
The lamps come on
with precocious nostalgia.
Crickets resume in the folds of darkness,
and a boat left empty at the dock
knocks in the negligible waves.
Others have stopped at a spot like this
to listen to a lake's consoling messages.
Through decades of summers
their lowered voices abide,
filtered through the subsequent silences
of love withheld,
or the lies administered
to small ongoing arguments
like fresh bandages, to soothe them.
We stood there too, in northern Wisconsin
in the steadiness of summer,
our children unborn,
our love for one another boundless.
Looking back now
into the vacant twilight of a snapshot,
a reach of fragrant lawn—
the ordinary present darkens
in the tinctures of the past.
But I would not go back to see
the Hotel du Nord loom up again,

its innocent porches, its balconies of hope,
knowing that the paths beside the lake
all lead here, to the one place.
There is no elsewhere.

Rhymes for Old Age

The wind's untiring saxophone
keens at the glass.
The lamp sheds a monochrome
of stainless steel and linens,
the nurse in her snowy dress
firm in her regimens.

The form in the bed
is a soul diminished
to a fledgling, fed
on the tentative balm of spring,
sketch for an angel, half-finished,
shoulder blades the stubs of wings.

Darkened with glaucoma,
the room floats on the retina.
The long vowel of *coma*
broods in the breath, part vapor.
What has become of the penetralia?
Eau de cologne sanctifies the diaper.

Flood and drag, the undertow.
One slips into it undressed,
as into first love, the vertigo
that shrinks to a keepsake of passion.
Sky's amethyst
lies with a sponge in the basin.

Paper White Narcissus

Awake or asleep,
the brain dreams at midnight,
roused by the furnace tenderly clanking,
or the errant perfume of the narcissus
forced from midwinter, hard as a kiss.

It dreams its goodbye
to the swindler at the door,
who turns into the granular snow light,
away. And goodbye, tense new hearts
into which the rough hand and its pallor
already have reached.
Grief makes its bouquet the hour
the fire-colored pollen starts to fall.

The wicked flowers of memory
are also white, and bloom anywhere.
Far away, in summer,
the pit loosens in the peach
and the ring slips off
into tall grass, and is lost.
Love comes to nothing.

Nectar dampens the starry clots
that the bees do not visit.
No loveliness, no fragrance or longing
brings on the black honey of forgetfulness
though grief is perennial.

Words for Synthesizer

When I first heard
what a machine could do with music,
I loved the wind a little less.
The trout still rose
through the clean mists
guarding childhood,
making their delicate splash,
but next to the meshing sugars
of a voice fed back to itself,
the splash diminished.

To tell the truth,
I miss the whisper in the mix,
near-kiss of mouth and microphone,
and the frictional slide
of fingers on the strings.
They were the first step
toward relinquishment.
But fish-splash and wind
and all loved things
come home to the black sound-box.

The mind's advice to itself
is brainwashing, and it works.
How else could I loll so easily
on the ladder of the years,
the calibrated loneliness

of growing up and old?
It's almost effortless,
now that I find distortion thrilling.

Abandoned House in Late Light

A sparrow lights
among the open cones
high in the white pine.
Then slips, a leaf
traveling the green ladders
down to the spiced humus,
which feeds on all things
missing, all things lost.
The cloven prints of deer,
a squirrel's immaculate spine,
and somewhere between
the wind and the gray leaves
a far-off waterfall
pours through the cold air,
dismantling a tree,
stripping away the bodies
that the souls may not
linger here among us.
The migrant orioles
disown the paintless birdhouse
vacant in the birch.
Pendulous with grapes, vines
scrawl across the lattice,
scattering raisins
darkened with wine
into the black breakdown of soil.
For years a neighbor swept
the long, cloud-colored

boards of his porch,
and the grit suspended,
like the sound of the ax
in the stacked wood.
Now he lives where even
the wind dissolves,
in a house of breathless passages,
the windows open to birds and snow,
a lock full of rust on the door.

Let *X*

Let *x* equal a birthday,
the point at which
the unknown segment of a life
attaches to the known.
Who wouldn't drive a little fast,
dosed with the moon and a red car,
having laughed past midnight
with another woman
about men, how simple they are,
how dangerous,
each one with his own translation,
imagination into love?

I think of the body before
and the body afterward,
its history of counterparts,
the thieves it housed,
the travelers.
A hand on my breast,
where none is now,
a mouth on my mouth,
summoned by the talk of minds
well versed in partial darkness,
the music beating in the radio,
the hazardous moonlit roads.

Electrical Storm

Beyond the rain
the carbon blue of evening also falls,
the dazzling, distant, wayward blue
of hope, of heaven,
of a lake for drowning.
Unallied to any sadness,
the full-blown lilacs
turn the color of windows,
their roots in scary shadow,
their flowers immortal.
Isn't it prediction
to say the seed
that hardens in a tree
is orphan seed? Or that
branches displaced by wind
are errant bits of destiny?
And does it matter
if it's the ornamental
pruned against doubling
that volunteers itself,
and not the whippet sapling,
the one with a tight life inside it?
Each image elected by the storm
might be the one clear-spoken sign:
the leaning barn, the tangled field,
the slur of the pale dust in my hand
where the aspirin were.
Ribbons of pallor illuminate

a sky of old newspapers,
unreadable dark print for which
there is no name or paraphrase.

The Colorless Center of Everything

At the center of the wet clay
lithe in the potter's hand
is the shape of the new bowl, invisible.
A cross section of the full spectrum
shows the same colorless zero
at the core, the point at which
all colors neutralize and vanish,
darken to extinction. All except violet,
the unreasonable color, the color of sex.
Thus we converse not in the
psychologically primary hues,
but in terra cotta, Egyptian green,
burnt sienna, cerise…

Peruvian lilies in a clay bowl
consist of primary pigments and light.
Inside each yellow flower stitched with red
the iridescent pollens cling,
alien dust the traveler brings
home with the long green stems.
The bowl is glazed blue-black.

Inside the woman's body
is the colorless center of marriage,
against which the man hardens himself.
The bowl of flowers is simply
his gift to her.
The third part is their subtext,

an emptiness complete in itself
like the space between them as they sleep,
or the night sky,
blue-black and monochromatic.
So that our lives resemble
the truculent harmonies in the prism,
but with black mixed in.

Translations from the Rational

The roofless houses by the roadside drown
in sky the color of Mercurochrome.
Greener than snow, the acres of limestone
force new beauty from a simple noun,
the last of the five elements: bone.
Without a place to rest, the remnant sounds
of aftermath pray to the empty towns
for resurrection of the chromosome.
The distant roses of plutonium
make of the sky a staggering bouquet
turned in upon itself, a cranium
packed with scenes from life, a matinee
of dreams for the millennium,
the lit terrain we called the Milky Way.

Across the bulging, dust-dark summer storm,
lightning prints a jagged, branching track.
Nostalgia's not a longing to go back,
nor love of the world a love of form.
Not quite. We glimpse another paradise
obscured by its protective colorations,
but lose it to a flux of short durations.
All that we love, we try to memorize.
Time undermines that love. Each tense collides,
a broken storm of many blossomings.
The nets we throw out drag the wayward tides
for things lost long ago to the water's rings.
We watch the speckled, paling undersides
of those quick fish, the vanishing evenings.

Partita for Solo Violin

What comes to mind is a pond
clotted with lilies, a black pond,
though the blackness may be
nothing more than afterthought
overlaid on the green water.
Lilacs break along the shore,
damp white clusters
throwing back starlight
and the smell of sleep.
In what world do I wake?

Snows sweep in to tranquilize
places disturbed by holiness.
The lilies withdraw,
and the ice forms a thick lens
through which I see
the candles of lost love
glimmering still.
But stars make a light
like that in the cold crystals
regardless of histories.

A hound mourns in the pine
undercurrents of the wind.
Lilies in cellophane.
The smell of the cutoff stems.
A host of whittling flames
illuminates the private shrines

and spills a cuneiform
queer as bird tracks on the snow.
A score for human voice,
a score for strings.

The charring sky lets fall
the first notes, showers of embers
spawned in the final black.
I forage in that night for them,
tracking the cool vestiges
far into silence.
Like the wasps I have built
a tenement of paper,
hole upon hole of storage,
the imaginer's emblem and home.

Surrounding currents bear away
this crude notation. It rides
on water dark with history,
not starlessness. I conceive of
a music crushed from earthly loves,
each note contributing
its lilacs, its snowbanks, its dead
dragged in the undertow. A music
composed of vital sparks, but played
with a plaintive, funereal coloring.

from

Perdido

1991

Why All Good Music Is Sad

Before I knew that I would die,
I lolled in the cool green twilight
over the reef, the hot sun on my back,
watching the iridescent schools
flick and glide among stone flowers,
and the lacy fans blow back and forth
in the watery winds of the underworld.
I saw the long, bright muscle of a fish
writhing on a spear, spasm and flash,
a music violent and gleaming,
abandoned to its one desire.
The white radiance of Perdido
filtered down through the rocking gloom
so that it was Perdido there too,
in that strange, stroking, half-lit world.
Before I knew that love
would end my willful ignorance of death,
I didn't think there was much
left in me that was virgin, but there was.
That's why all good music is sad.
It makes the sound of the end before the end,
and leaves behind it
the ghost of the part that was sacrificed,
a chord to represent the membrane,
broken only once, that keeps the world away.
That's how the fish became the metaphor:
one lithe and silvery life impaled,
fighting death with its own failing beauty,

thrashing on the apex of its fear.
Art was once my cold solace,
the ice pack I held to love's torn body,
but that was before I lay
as if asleep above the wavering reef,
or saw the barbed spear strike the fish
that seemed for an instant to be
something outside myself, before I knew
that the sea was my bed and the fish was me.

A Minor Crush of Cells

I thought that the earth
would be the last thing that I loved,
the first and the last,

but there were many loves beyond it,

things I did not at first
know that I loved.

Children, for example,
though they no longer had much gravity,

would come sometimes
out onto the dusty, twilit sidewalks
to play their eternal games.

I remember the chalk's soft scraping.

It's not nostalgia, this hybrid sadness,
not the fragile boat that rides

the swift indwelling currents
into worlds that exclude
the loved things from each previous world,

though like nostalgia its halves
are always enemies, in this case
sex and death.

I look up into the night's faint green,
up into the pierced smoke of heaven,
and am for a moment

nothing but a minor crush of cells,

a bit of human substance
playful in imaginary forms.

Gravity draws down to me a halo
whipped up of holy dust

or dust from outer space:
dim chalk of moonlight, phosphor,

youth in the eyes of my former selves.

The Givens

One side of the dialogue
I have by heart,
but learned it so long ago
each phrase seems
sullenly dangerous now, in that
it withholds something I once knew.
The words go forth,
sleek pigeons into the wild sky,
smaller and smaller and smaller,
like pictures trapped in a telescope,
shrinking it-ward segment by segment.

I had as a child a mind
already rife with sacred greens
I could neither harvest nor ignore.
They sprang up everywhere:
from the black dirt of memory—
the old farm, its raspberries
diamonded with dew, etc.—
even from bodiless fantasy,
and from the mailbox full of letters
standing in for the various
emotions and kinds of news.

Part of myself must have
courted and married another part.
I don't know when it happened.
I know I heard both voices early on.

But one now drags its half of the duet
off into a scary song about
its intimations of the time ahead:
love, lost love, and love again,
and I dislike the long-drawn,
melancholy music that it makes.

But it's beautiful here
in this house above the valley,
close to the crumpled
paper of the clouds.
Birds return from invisible worlds.
Their feet print words on my sills.
And words weigh down the long,
soft-spoken branches of the evergreens,
weigh the unpruned
branches of abandoned orchards
down into the blond grass
where the pears,
grown small and hard with wildness,
soften and disappear.

And yet,
sometimes sick of the orderly,
pallid little stars,
I hear the stray heart's careless noise,
its tears and mysteries of laughter
close outside. It calls to me,
that voice, its ragged sweetness
intimate with everything I fear.

Dream of the Interior

A dog that has been sleeping on a crypt
rouses and stands up, her yellow hide

sunken over the haunches,
pendant teats crusted and dry.

Green spotted lizards drop noisily
down through the serrated leaves,

rustling among the wooden crosses,
plastic flowers, and melted votive stubs,

the heaped sand bordered by shells.
What do I long for or deny such that

I dream up this paradise for myself,
and why is there so much death in it,

so many nameless grave-dunes?
Beyond the tumbled coral wall,

the heavy sea-grapes hang in dust,
the sea folds up its white rags

and shakes them out again,
and the crude oars of the fishermen

dip and rise and fling away
their sapphire droplets.

If I leave this place, could I find my way
home through the streets of sand,

the bones asleep in the heat?
A vine like honeysuckle scribbles

over the wall, one sweet taste
on the pale green tip of each stigma,

the delicately splayed petals spilling
pale orange dust and perfume.

If I put my tongue to a single flower,
I'd suspend here forever

in my unknown need,
swaying like the black dog

on his yellow bride, slightly off balance
among the dead, locked in a dream.

Window in the Shape of a Diamond

Our room in the hotel was dark
except for a narrow slash of afternoon
containing a twig of orange leaves,
an empty field, and far away,
mountains in a pitch-blue sky.
Hour upon hour we lay,
the sheets kicked free,
watching the little landscape flare
in final colors of foreclosure,
as perfectly displaced
as the delicately tinted paper scenes
inside the hollow sugar eggs
that kids devour at Easter.
Beloved is a word concealing
four sharp points,
four kinds of innocence,
four winds of change.
One look inside it
and the world abruptly petrifies
into another of its
small cold monuments.

The Shades of Grand Central

You could tell that the flowers
splayed in the vendors' buckets

had come from the hothouse factories

lit all night to force more blooms.
Among the blue and scarlet flames
the eyes of the homeless flicked

from no one to no one,
and the name for them came to me
sharp in the winter dark

as if it had always been a word.

I climbed the heavy stairs
up out of the pit that steams
and quakes with machine life,

past flowers for the lover
and the lonely self,

flowers for the longtime dead and for
the fresh-cut holes in the frozen hill,

and for all the children
locked out of the world,

including my own,
about whom I know nothing,

not even how many, not even their names,

which are like thin ice and do not bear
the weight of my wondering about them.

I came up into the purifying cold,

the small, stinging arrows of snow,
and when I turned my head against it

I saw the hulk of a Dumpster
out back of a rib house, in an alley.
A man in a hooded burlap robe

had led his flock of vagrant dogs to food.

What is an individual grief
but a flake in the storm?

He threw to the dogs the gnawed-on ribs
the restaurant had thrown away.

Snow diffused the harsh
halo of the streetlamp and lit
the folds of his strange apparel.

The dog bodies took each rib with a seizure,
white-backed and ravenous.

Useless Islands

I'm trying to remember
what happened when love overtook me,

how the old self slipped
from its hard boundaries

like a ripe plum out of its skin.
It's a personal mystery.

It was August, each moment
setting fire to the next,

the woods already
bloodied by the first bright deaths.

I'm trying to remember, but there's
a blacked-out part to the story,

a steep, crashing wall of seawater,
a long thrill of fear. I was dragged

in an undertow as if out of sleep,
and the blue-green light I swam toward

was this paradise of islands,
these green days spilled

across a vast mercurial blue.
We lie in a flood of white sand

under the broken prism of the sky,
watching its fragile rays disappear

down the secretive avenues of palms.
How long can we lie here?

The luminous charcoal and manila clouds
cross like fish overhead.

His hand sleeps on my thigh.
The ratcheted voices of the tree frogs

start up their random music,
and we lie listening. It's a way

of passing more slowly through,
of dragging a stick in the water

like a brake. There's the dull
clop of goats on the red dirt road,

and the lisp of the sand beneath us.
What the leaves were saying

back in the other life,
the palms are saying here.

It's the words to the long slow sad
familiar hymn about the hourglass.

I lie beside my love
in the silence between two waves,

the grains of my body pouring.
I know that the second wave will ripen

and fall. It will fall in a world
that is emerald and sapphire,

lit by the sparks of the sea. A world
that will darken and abandon me.

The Condom Tree

Pleasure must slip
right through memory's barbed wire,
because sex makes lost things reappear.
This afternoon when I shut my eyes
beneath his body's heavy braille,
I fell through the rosy darkness
all the way back to my tenth year,
the year of the secret
place by the river,
where the old dam spilled
long ropes of water and the froth
chafed the small stones smooth.
I looked up and there it was,
a young maple
still raw in early spring,
and drooping pale
from every reachable branch
dozens of latex blooms.
I knew what they were,
that the older kids
had hung them there,
but the tree—was it beautiful,
caught in that dirty floral light,
or was it an ugly thing?
Beautiful first, and ugly afterward,
when I saw up close
the shriveled human skins?
That must be right,

though in the remembering
its value has been changed again,
and now that flowering
dapples the two of us
with its tendered shadows,
dapples the rumpled bed as it slips
out of the damp present
into our separate pasts.

Six Belons

The ruckled lips gaped slightly, but when
I slipped the knife in next to the hinge,
they closed to a stone.
The violence it took to unlock them!
Each wounded thing lay in opalescent milk
like an albino heart,
muscle sliced from the roof-shell.
I took each one pale and harmless
into my mouth and held it there,
tasting the difference between
the ligament and the pure, faintly
coffee-colored flesh that was unflinching
even in the acid of lemon juice,
so that I felt I was eating
not the body but the life in the body.
Afterward my mouth stayed greedy
though it carried the sea-rankness
away with it, a taste usually transient,
held for a moment beyond its time
on mustache or fingertip.
The shells looked abruptly old,
crudely fluted, gray-green, flecked
with the undersea equivalent of lichens,
and pearly, slick, bereft of all their meat.
The creatures themselves were gone,
the succulent indecent briny ghosts
that caused this arousal, this feeding,
and now a sudden loneliness.

Chanel No. 5

Life had become a sort of gorgeous elegy,
intimate with things about to be lost.

The waiter's hand on the wineglass
seemed an intermediary flame,

the atoms rampant inside it,

though it moved slowly
and hesitated slightly
before it was withdrawn

as if it meant to ask
whether anything more was wanted.

Abstracted by the static of the surf,

I dined alone, the beach hotel
half empty in the off-season,

the honeymooning couple
at the table next to mine

caressing with their voices
the still-folded map of their future,

their two armies still in reserve,

the flowers massed between them
a flimsy barricade
against their wakening grief.

The long pin of her corsage
pierced the thin silk on her breast:
white flower, green leaf, black dress.

In her perfume I smelled
the residue of all their recent happiness,
a sweetness corrupted by the sea, and yet

she wore it innocently, that target.

It was a fledgling bitterness I caught
off a shred of air that had touched her dress
as she rose to follow her husband-mystery.

The little emblem inside the flame,
the male and female become one,

was blackening back in their room

overlooking the sea, but before they
hurried back to it, she looked at me,
and, as if to inoculate herself against me,

inclined her head to smell her own gardenia.

The Blade of Nostalgia

When fed into the crude, imaginary
machine we call the memory,

the brain's hard pictures
slide into the suggestive
waters of the counterfeit.

They come out glamorous and simplified,

even the violent ones,
even the ones that are snapshots of fear.

Maybe those costumed,
clung-to fragments are the first wedge

nostalgia drives into our dreaming.

Maybe our dreams are corrupted
right from the start: the weight

of apples in the blossoms overhead.

Even the two thin reddish dogs
nosing down the aisles of crippled trees,
digging in the weak shade

thrown by the first flowerers,

snuffle in the blackened leaves
for the scent of a dead year.

Childhood, first love, first loss of love—

the saying of their names
brings an ache to the teeth
like that of tears withheld.

What must happen now
is that the small funerals
celebrated in the left-behind life

for their black exotica, their high relief,

their candles and withered wreaths,
must be allowed to pass through
into the sleeping world,

there to be preserved and honored
in the fullness and color of their forms,

their past lives their coffins.

Goodbye then to all innocent surprise
at mortality's panache,
and goodbye to the children fallen

ahead of me into the slow whirlpool
I conceal within myself, my death,

into its snow-froth and the green-black
muscle of its persuasion.

The spirits of children
must look like the spirits of animals,
though in the adult human

the vacancy left by the child
probably darkens the surviving form.

The apples drop their blossom-shadows
onto the still-brown grass.
Old selves, this is partly for you,

there at the edge of the woods
like a troop of boy soldiers.

You can go on living with the blade
of nostalgia in your hearts forever,
my pale darlings. It changes nothing.

Don't you recognize me? I admit
I, too, am almost invisible now, almost.

Like everything else, I take on
light and color from outside myself,
but it is old light, old paint.

The first shadows are supple ones,
school of gray glimpses, insubstantial.

In children, the quality of darkness
changes inside the sleeping mouth,

and the ghost of child-grime—
that infinite smudge of no color—

blows off into the afterlife.

Revenge

He was standing on the hotel balcony
when I awoke, watching the late afternoon

sluice down green-gold
over the fronds of the royal palms.

Palms in wind make a sound
like knives being sharpened,

languorous in my dispersing sleep,
slice-slicing against themselves.

He was watching the melon-colored light
run over the slow swells,

and the pleasure boats trailing
their long white creamy wakes,

their engines shuddering.
My waking thought was that

I was waking *inside a century,*
a cage bigger than our lives,

and that the freedom to roam around in it
was an illusion we both had, or an irony

we'd once abided by but had forgotten,
walking in the drifting dunes of light,

the snows of Perdido, snows of crushed coral,
on the edge of the trespassing sea.

The sheets were imprinted on my skin.
The cool air fingered each crease

and the fresh grass matting felt
pleasingly harsh and raw underfoot.

No one could see me
there in the palm shadows, naked

and dappled by the sun's warm camouflage.
The passing seconds were almost visible,

a faintly glamorous stream of light
that flowed over the moving boats,

brightened the frictional leaves.
He put his arm around my shoulders,

the smell of the day in his shirt,
so that his thumb not quite touched

my nipple, which shriveled,
and with the other hand slowly

unbuttoned and unzipped himself,
all the while watching the pleasure boats

glide past us trailing bits of broken mirror,
their engines pulsing steadily,

fueled by what's left of the future.

Word Silence

There's a flame like the flame of fucking
that longs to be put out: words are filings
drawn toward a vast magnetic silence.
The loins ask their usual question
concerning loneliness.
The answer is always a mountaintop
erasing itself in a cloud.
It's as if the mind keeps flipping
a coin with a lullaby on one side
and a frightening thrill on the other,
and if it lands it's
back in the air at once.
A word can rub itself rosy
against its cage of context,
starting a small fire in the sentence
and trapping for a moment
the twin scents of now and goodbye.
The sexual mimicry always surprises me:
the long dive the talky mind makes
into the pleasures of its native dark.
Like pain, such joy is locked
in forgetfulness, and the prisoner
must shout for freedom again and again.
Is that what breaks the sentences apart
and spreads their embers in a cooling silence?
The pen lies in the bleach of sunlight
fallen on the desk, ghost-sheet of a bed
turned back. If I look for a long time

into its wordlessness, I can see
the vestiges of something that I knew
dissolving. Something that I no longer know.
And there I sleep like an innocent
among the words I loved
but crushed for their inflammable perfumes.

O Miami

Wherever the cloth of my dress touched me
it seemed a hand was about to touch me.
The dark drew heat from my skin,
a mild sunburn that made the palm of my hand
itch in his, and my feet chafe
in the cool sugary sand, the wave-froth.
Miami weltered in the wakes of speedboats,
its lights pink-silver, smeared across the bay.
We paid two dollars to walk on the pier,
its long eroded sticky boards,
past the spigots and the crude scaling tables
to the end where a man shone a flashlight
into the tangled glitter of his tackle box.
Below us the water rocked and smashed.
I tugged the tails of his shirt
out of his pants and slipped both hands
up the ladder of his back,
for which he opened a look at me
that made the muscles of my body swim
like a school of quick fish, flinching as one,
rising to feed in water that was mirror-clean
and empty, deep, abstract.
Among them gleamed the bright hook,
the hook that drags death into the story,
the idea of death which starts so barbed and small.
The man laid a catfish out on the rough wood,
and pierced its skull with an awl.
Tore the lure from the gristly tissue of the lips.

Across the bay, the city spilled its languid neons.
His heart beat under my hand.
Every muscle was a fish in the shoal,
and every act from that point on
an act of defiance: his mouth on my throat,
my hand in his salty hair, so that
when he turned the key in the hotel room door
I was already stepping out of my sandals.
The maid had turned down the bed.
Every muscle was a fish. I heard my own voice
cry out *O Miami*, words he took from me.
The water-sound was loud in the palmy dark,
and the sound the fish made beating
the rough boards with its flagrant silver tail.
The hook sinks down through the dream of love.
The moment of greeting is the moment of farewell.

from

The Ghost of Eden

1995

Animal Graves

The mower flipped it belly up,
a baby garter less than a foot long,
dull green with a single sharp

stripe of pale manila down its back,
same color as the underside,
which was cut in two places,

a loop of intestine poking out.

It wouldn't live,
so I ran the blade over it again,

and cut it again but didn't kill it,

and again and then again,
a cloud of two-cycle fuel smoke
on me like a swarm of bees.

It took so long
my mind had time to spiral
back to the graveyard

I tended as a child
for the dead ones, wild and tame:
fish from the bubbling green aquarium,

squirrels from the road,
the blue jay stalked to a raucous death
by Cicero the patient, the tireless hunter,

who himself was laid to rest
one August afternoon
under a rock painted gray, his color,

with a white splash for his white splash.

Once in the woods I found the skeleton
of a deer laid out like a diagram,

long spine curved
like a necklace of crude, ochre spools
with the string rotted away,

and the dull metal shaft of the arrow
lying where it must have pierced

not the heart, not the head,
but the underbelly, the soft part
where the sex once was.

I carried home the skull
with its nubs of not-yet-horns
which the mice had overlooked,

and set it on a rock
in my kingdom of the dead.

Before I chopped the little snake
to bits of raw mosaic,

it drew itself
into an upward-straining coil,
head weaving, mouth open,

hissing at the noise that hurt it.

The stripe was made
of tiny paper diamonds,
sharp-edged but insubstantial,

like an X-ray of the spine
or the ghost beginning to pull away.

What taught the snake to make itself
seem bigger than it was,
to spend those last few seconds

dancing in the roar
and shadow of its death?

Now I see, though none exists,
its grave:

harebells withered in a jar,
a yellow spiral
painted on a green-black stone,

a ring of upright pinecones for a fence.
That's how the deer skull lay in state

until one of the neighborhood dogs
came to claim it,

and carried it off to bury
in the larger graveyard of the world.

The Pools

I used to look into the green-brown
pools of the Ausable, the places
where the pouring cold slowed,

and see a mystery there.
I called it God for the way
it made my heart feel crushed

with love for the world outside myself,

each stone distinct and magnified,
trembling in the current's thick lens.

Now when I can't sleep
I say as a prayer
the names of all the little brooks,

Slide and Gill and Shadow,
and the names of the river pools
I fished at dusk,

working my way upstream through
slow sliding eddies and buckets of froth:

the flume, the bend, Hull's Falls, the potholes.
It's like saying the names
of the dead and the missing—

the Ausable, the Boquet, the Opalescent—

though their waters still
rush down over the gray ledges
toward Lake Champlain.

The flume was always
full of bark-colored shadows,

shafts of green light fallen
from the pines, and the silver swirls

of rising trout where now
the gray-fleshed hatchery fish
feed on the damaged magic.

Sleepless, I call to mind
the high granite walls
scored in the thaws,

the banks of black-stemmed ferns.

I lie again on a warm rock
and feel the hand of God on my back,

and feel it withdraw
in the exact instant the sun
withdraws its treasure from the water—

a tiny dissonance,
like bad news forgotten for a moment
but the shadow of its anxiety holding on,

making a little cloud of its own.

It was the thing outside the human
that I loved, and the way

I could enter it,
the muscle-ache of diving

down into the cold, green-brown spangles,

myself a part of the glimmering blur,
the falling coins of light.

Scraps of that beauty survive
in the world here and there—

sparks of rain in the pine candles,
a leaf turning in underwater currents,

then lost in the smoke of faster water.

Sometimes I glimpse the future
in the evenings. It appears
like a doe on silencing moss,

foraging among pocked leaves,
drinking the last light in the pools.

It doesn't even raise its head
to look at me. I'm not a danger to it,

trapped as I am in the purely human.

Little Snowscape

Consciousness ends, says the snow,
and in the meantime it's a window
left open in winter—

the cold is the same inside and out.

The great tracts of dreamland
stretch away under the vanishing balsams.

It's that point in the afternoon
when the sparks in the fresh contours

begin to go out, and shadow flakes
darken the falling air.

I'm an animal
shivering in the Godlike glitter,

the burial of earth by light
and then by light's extinction.

I want to eat, like the cold shadow,
and to be eaten, like the cold brightness.
They are my parents.

Already my tracks fill with a numb blue,

the little steps I've taken across the blur,
the white concealment,
my lies to myself.

I stand on the seam between two worlds
and think I'll never have to choose between

this one and the dead one.

My cells are made of this one,
so if it continues, I continue.
But when I look up I see that the snow

falls from a fountain that is not immortal.

The Ruiner of Lives

Who knows how things end up
spliced together in the mind.

Last night the car was lugging
up the long hill toward home
when a fox came sleepwalking

out of the alders onto the road.
Something was wrong with it.
It listed a little to one side

and moved without fox-quickness,
not sniffing, not scared,
but calm, almost formal,

with a yellow opacity in its eyes

as if it had recently
been dreaming of being blind.

It stood staring down the double barrel
of the headlights till I stopped the car.

Who knows why, but at that moment
five words came awake in my mind:

God the ruiner of lives—

a line of graffiti I once saw
sprayed on a pink wall in the tropics.
Now five sharp stars in a northern night,

shaken out of their sleep.

It was only August, but already
the uppermost leaves of the stricken maples
were ragged and red,

and the small curled leaves
of the barren apples
skittered across the road.

The fox and I—who was our ruiner?

I with the sin of despair
for the world my species has spoiled,

the fox with its hunger,
its rabies, its dirty coat
slung over a frail skeleton.

A fox of the future
digging in the underbrush
for our remains will find

more trash than bones.

I laid my hand over my heart
to put out the fire lit by this idea,
and stroked and stroked as if it were

a terrorist I could cure of its rage
with kindness and animal calm.

The yellow eyes went on dreaming
the car, the road curved into the dark.

Poor fox, poor mystic,
attracted to a light it can't explain.

A light that drives away,
and leaves us both
here under the cold,

crumbling trees of heaven.

The Immortal Pilots

The noise throws down
twin shadows, hunting shadows
on a black joyride.

They roar up the silver vein of the river
and out over the stony peaks,

which have been shrunk to a luminous
green musculature on their screens.
Who are the pilots, too high to see

the splayed hearts of deer tracks

under the apple trees, or smell
the cider in the fallen fruit?

Who are the vandals that ransack
the wilderness of clouds?

Below them, a thin froth of waterfall
spills from a rock face.
They see its sudden wreckage,

its yielding gouts,

and the wind tear into the papery
leaves of the poplars, roughing them up

so the undersides show—
a glimpse of paleness

like a glimpse of underwear.

The pilots are young men,
and still immortal.

Already in the cold
quadrants of their hearts
they imagine the whole world

flowering beneath them. It feels
like love, like being with a woman
who flowers beneath them,

so that they wonder
how it would feel to go on
riding the young green world that way,

to a climax of spectral light.

Snow in Condoland

I enter the orchard at nightfall
when it's hard to tell
the clots of late spring snow

from the apple blossoms,
the dead from the living,

though the mind has no trouble
with snow as a flower,
snow as a corsage

it can press inside its heavy book.
I could go on turning the pages
forever, so vivid

are the images there,
so perfectly preserved.
Their forms grow vaguer in the yards

as the slow light falls on swing sets,

paved culs-de-sac, mailboxes,
doghouses, acres of cold cars,
the whole stilled ocean of roofs.

The orchard has been gone
for a decade, and still the sentences
push through the laden branches,

into each frozen complex
of white on white.

It fascinates me,
the way language smudges and erases
and redraws what it wants for itself.

Even now the apples
are ripening somewhere,

inside the cold petals maybe,
in the dark, still-infant part,

where a faint pink fever
was once suppressed.

Bad Movie, Bad Audience

Matinees are the best time
for bad movies—squad cars
spewing orange flame, the telephone

dead in the babysitter's hand.
Glinting with knives and missiles,

men stalk through the double
wilderness of sex and war

all through the eerie
fictions of the afternoon.
The audience is restless,

a wicked ocean roughing up its boats.

It makes a noise I seem to need.
The ruby bracelet

clinks against the handcuff,
all the cars make squealing sounds.
The kid in front of me

wants more candy,
rocks in her velvet seat. *Shut up,*

says her mother, maybe seventeen.
Just shut the fuck up.

The corpses of the future
drift across the galaxy with nothing
in their stiff, irradiated hands.

In our ears the turbo revs,
the cheekbone cracks,
a stocking slithers to the floor.

Cocteau said film is death at work.

Out of the twilight
a small voice hisses

Shut up, just shut the fuck up.

The Devil I Don't Know

It seems to be the purpose of mourning

to change the mourner, to tip over,
in the end, the urn that holds the grief.

When a loved person dies,
elegy formalizes that work.

But what if it's the holy thing itself,
the thing beseeched with prayer,
that's the deceased? What good is elegy then?

I was pushing my cart through the sharp
fluorescence of the supermarket,

lost in this question. People pawed
through the shrink-wrapped meats,

which look like body parts to me
since I stopped eating them,

things that should have been buried,

and I thought, *To what should I pray?*
I'd always prayed to the ineffable
in its body the earth,

to the sacred violence of storms,
huge tracts of seaweeds rocked in the dark,

the icy crystals of the stars above the snow,
the mystery untamable and pure.

So what should I pray to now
in the hour of my abandonment?

Should I stand in my shining cart and shout
that the age of darkness is upon us?

Or turn inward to the old disciplines
and wander like a disembodied soul
through the wreckage, honoring my vows,

faithful to the end? A pilgrim
grown bright and clean as a flame,

eating only the gifts of the plants
and trees, what fattens among leaves

or swells in the soil underfoot?
Pure offerings. That means

no to fellow creatures bloated with steroids,

no to the heavy metals that shine
in the mackerel like tarnished silver,

no to the black-veined shrimp
in their see-through shells.

No to the embalming liquids
injected with needles,

no to the little chops packaged in rows
like a litter of stillborn puppies,

no to the chicken's sputum-colored
globules of fat, no to the devil I know.

The circular blade started up in the deli,

pink sheets of ham drooping into the plastic
glove of the man behind the counter.

What am I, an empty vessel waiting
for some new holy thing to come pour itself
into me? Where is the new divine?

I want to feed myself
into the machines of grief

and come out changed, transformed,
a new soul with a new consciousness.

I want a new inscrutable to worship,

to turn to in times of uncertainty and fear.
But there's only
the soft hiss of the lobster tank,

and the one surviving lobster, just sold,
waving its pegged claws from the scale.

A small swordfish gleams behind the glass.
Dear higher power, dear corpse of the world

gutted, garnished, laid out on ice.

The Whirlpool

Someone at the party said it was impossible
to imagine the death of the species

(the cocktails sparkling and the voices
murmuring together of life's tenacity),

but I could imagine it.

I stood looking down from the balcony
at the Hudson's starved and beaten ghost,
the high walls of the stone canyons

still catching light
though the big flame of the day was guttering.

A voice said, *Sure, the dinosaurs died.*
But they still roam the pristine world

and thrash their spiny tails in our imaginations,
don't they? That's a kind of life.

The city below me kept folding
in on itself in a sickening swirl,
the lines of traffic

feeding through the intersections
like the wild spirals of DNA, red and white
(their lights in the dusk just coming on).

It was like looking into the head of a peony
vivid with ants, stemless,

a skull with its innards devoured,

all shell, all aftermath,
white in places like driftwood or bone,
though I didn't say that.

I can hear the voices of the dead out here,

murmuring together of life's fragility.
Drawn by the density of human sound,

they turn around us in a slow wheel,
though we are not their center of gravity.
What a whirling paradise this is,

this suck of conscious seconds

drawing me into the day's black ending,
and far below me the city's crawling stars,

each one a second in the dream.

Touch-me-not

I have to fight in myself the desire
to put down the pen and go outside
where the tufted, seed-heavy grasses

float on the slow river of August.

When a poem touches on the act of writing,
it breaks the dream. That's why this one
opens as it does—defensive,

already split between wanting to know
where it's going and wanting not to know.

I lie down under the sketchy canopy
of the field with my face close
to the cellar smell of earth

where the white shoots gleam
doubled up in the dew
in their little preserve.

I'd rather watch the bees
work the wildflowers

than follow the cursive tracks
wherever it is they go.
Something, maybe the soul,

says language is a whip that hurts it,

slicing open the still-forming
sky-colored chicory flowers,
leaving the flayed stems to say

what the truth is.
I'd rather listen to the brook,

its words always garbled
just out of earshot.

It's not the words themselves
that scare the soul,
but their unearthly gleam,

the gleam the pallbearers follow
first to the church
and then to the hole in the ground.

One day what has always been true
will no longer be true, just like that.

If this were a poem about my own death,
I'd know how to make the rasp and honey
of the August field take on that meaning,

and I'd rest for a while in the image
of my body married to the black
beloved dirt, the microbes, the rains,

the weed seeds sending out
their slender filaments of root.

But it's not my death that's set
like a steel trap at the end of the poem.
It's the earth's, upon whose body I lie,

and toward whom the ant-trails of ink all lead.

This world has always been widow and widower,
the one we leave bereft

when we slip into the place
without sunlight, without leaves.
Now what has always been true

is no longer true. I want to lie down
and swim in the shade with the trout lilies
to avoid saying it.

The earth as it has always been
is saying its goodbyes. Another world

will overrun the emptiness,

but I love this one.
I let it hold me longer than I mean to,
the feather-leaves of yarrow,

the vetches' frail tendrils,
and the spotted touch-me-nots

that give such an intimate response
if you touch one of the tiny swollen pods—

faintly striped, fat in the middle,
and containing a tense spring,
an unspiraling release

that flings the seeds in all directions.
I touch, and between my fingers

the miniature violence spends itself.

Like the seeds I'm propelled
toward some future field,

which glows from far off
like the idea of plutonium,
immortal and alien.

When I hear the wind taking leave
of the stricken trees—the beeches,
the birches, the red spruce—

or the wet-rag-on-glass sound of the phoebe

in her nest of lichens under the eaves,
when I walk in the ferns' green perfume

or lie with my face among cool roots
and sprouts all intertangled and doomed,

I'm imagining what will happen
to the soul in me,

which feeds on these things,
and which I fear will go on living

after the loved world dies.

A Seduction

I had a dream so pure of form
it slipped intact from the dark:

out of a narrow cleft in granite,
a waterfall sluiced
down through damp mosses, lichens,

ferns in a glitter of thrown drops.

(I used to fish for trout shadows
there, in childhood,

where the partridgeberry trailed
its small green disks in the spray.)

But I was inside, looking out through
a crude window, a hole
in the wall of massive stones,

and saw the lit candles
overflowing on the ledge,

the long lily petals,
gray-edged and shrunken,
dropping onto the black crepe.

It was a place of remembrance
for the dead, and I thought:

The jewels in the brook
are the lights of grief.
The beloved is already dead:

all the green frailties
and sacramental waters

before the naked species
came to feed on them,

and the virulent armies went forth
leaking excrement and fuel
to colonize the last shreds of paradise.

O beautiful window cut from the dark.

In the moment of death
can I climb through the bright rectangle
into the resurrection,

a heaven preserved within myself?

I've lost the way.
O dream, come back for me.

The City in the Lilac

Early evening is lilac time,
when the stinging insects of memory

are drawn to the heavy, half-opened
flames. I put my face into a cluster

and breathe in the purple ether.

Some memories won't sleep,
even though there's nothing left of them

but the clipped twigs of hope,
the kid sticking her face into a flower,

feeling the hard little buds of sadness

forming under her shirt, a boy's shirt.
Nothing left but a feeling, an intimation

that the world is still spoiled in secret,
that no one sees it happen.

The perfume is inside the lilac's privacy.

It can lead you to a hideout,
a fort in the leaves,
but it can also trick you and go instead

down the stairs into the purple darkness

if you're not careful, if you're still
innocent, if you're ten years old

and the man taking your picture
against the bruise-colored velvet
shows you how the color becomes you,

shows you the secret room with the sliding
door, the tiny red night-light,

the beautiful lady rising
out of the cloudy chemicals of her bath
with nothing on, so that you can see close up

the black triangle between her legs,

its tufted fur, and her face, tense and proud.
It was Mrs. M from down the street.

But tonight the lilac doesn't smell
like the darkroom. It smells
like the melting honey of the candles

at the child's memorial, the tomboy

still in the photographer's costume,
a man's shirt, its tails
grazing the small thighs on which

a few tiny dots of blood still cling,

like the ones left on my own thighs
by the whip-sting of raspberry vines

when I went into the rough field
to smell the lilacs, and came away with

tonight's long scratch of childhood.

Inside the flower there's a black
honeycomb of rooms,

and in one of them a woman sleeps
lightly on a child's bed, dreaming
she has forgotten to lock the door,

which is soft, like a petal, and damaged.

An insect has eaten a hole in it.
It's keeping the woman separate
from the things that are already dead,

though she could see them looking in at her
if she opened her eyes. The room is lit

only by the evening sky, a faint rectangle
of window high above the city's

click and flash, its artificial moons,

its lights signaling red—you can't go.
Okay now you can go.

But go silently, go secretly.

White Conclusion

What's left of the day
leaks from an orange fissure overhead,

not the scorched hole
that scientists say is there
above the sunset, but a gash

in the carbon dreamscape of sky.

The other hole I imagine
to be white rimmed,

crusted with chemical ice

the color of fat or cancer cells,
or the froth at the mouth of a fox.

The sunset is only
tonight's unfinished watercolor

hiding the wound.
I see the gleam of weaponry in it,

far-off traffic and trash.
It's beautiful anyway,

the lacerated wilderness,

its faintening mauve above the uncut field
where the common flowers bloom as always,
live coals of hawkweed,

the vetches purple, near-invisible,
having soaked up some of the dusk.

And the white ones,
big multiplying clusters of them—

yarrow's coarse lace
and the sharp-edged daisies
growing even out of the stones in the wall.

Their white is a white that will survive us.

The Rule of the North Star

I should be ashamed to love
the first hard frost the way I do,

the way it glitters
over the surface of everything,

erasing whatever's human.

But I'm not. So I stand for a minute
in the crystalline grass
with an armload of frozen firewood,

letting a little of the ruthlessness
enter my bones, breathing
white sparrows into the air.

Oh, I know where the logic leads.
If the lights of the town

spoil the dark... If the trucks
downshifting on the Cascade hill
infect the wind...

If humanity's the enemy, the enemy is me.

But there's something in me, an arrow
that points toward wilderness,

toward the mountain that governs
such loves, its ledges high enough
to have caught last night's

faint halo of snow.
Wherever I am, in all weathers,
I look up, and it's there,

it always has been, rising even
above the charred towers of cities,
under the North Star, which glints down

onto its sharp summit,
and onto each withered grass blade,

each rattling pod, each burned-out car,
each smaller star of broken glass.

The mountain which has no name
burns in the distance

with a beautiful, radical plainness,

ledges bright with snowmelt.
It's the shrine,

the afterimage of the moment in which
I first imagined the world's death,

and knew at the same stroke
that though it would survive in some form,

it would not survive in this form.

The firewood aches in my arms.
Its smoke will cross over,

touching both the ash in the fireplace
and the face of the mirage.

The North Star
comes out earlier each evening.

It shines down onto the cloudy
or snowy or clear-skied world,

the wars, the droughts, the famines,

the ethnic cleansings,
just as it shone on the plagues,

the witch trials, the forced marches,
the purges, the great extinctions.

It will still be the sharpest spark
in the heavens long after my death,

your death, the next death of language—

a spark that will preside over the world
we leave behind, where acres of bones

catch the starlight, and a gray wind
scribbles in the drifts of ash.

Aisle of Dogs

In the first cage
a hunk of raw flesh.
No, it was alive, but skinned.

Or its back was skinned.
The knobs of the spine

poked through the bluish meat.

It was a pit bull, held by the shelter
for evidence until the case
could come to trial,

then they'd put him down. The dog,
not the human whose cruelty

lived on in the brindled body,
unmoving except for the enemy eyes.

Not for Adoption, said the sign.

All the other cages held adoptable pets,
the manic yappers, sad matted mongrels,
the dumb slobbering abandoned ones,

the sick, the shaved, the scratching,
the wounded and terrified, the lost,

one to a cage, their water dishes
overturned, their shit tracked around

on both sides of a long echoey
concrete aisle—clank of chain-mesh gates,
the attendant hosing down the gutters

with his headphones on, half-dancing
to the song in his head.

I'd come for kittens. There were none.
So I stood in front of the pit bull's
quivering carcass, its long-drawn death,

its untouched food, its incurable hatred
of my species, until the man with the hose
touched my arm and steered me away,

shaking his head in a way that said
Don't look. Leave him alone.
I don't know why, either.

Ghost Birches

The road crew worked all afternoon
cutting the dead birches.

Runoff from the road salt killed them,

trapped as they were on the narrow strip
left between the asphalt and the lake,

and rain-weakened. The acid
starts the yellow inflammation early,

the leaves in June already
arthritic in the cells.

We used to call them snow ghosts:

one white hidden in another.
Now they're stacked in six-foot sections,
the branches trimmed away,

and in the lake
the new emptiness heals over.

Then comes the plow of winter
straight down the valley,

pushing its wedge-shaped shadow.
All the lesser shadows move aside

as if still talking to one another,

flexible in wind, assessing their losses,
the future already upon them,

its sky-blue speckled crystals burning
down through the packed snow into the earth.

Maybe a man on the crew
with a truck of his own

will come on Saturday
to haul away the white logs, cut and split
and stack them, and he'll find them

crumbled to embers in his stove
when he comes home late and cold
from plowing after a heavy snow,

their shadows having already slipped
up the chimney to join all the other

shades of the world, the young ones
gone back to lie beside their stumps,

the old ones free to travel anywhere.

Silver Slur

Nothing stays attached to what I saw,

what I glimpsed from a train.
It has no magnet for meaning.

Four men sat on a wall shooting up,

companionable. One waved at me.
Waved the needle. Ten feet away,

a man was fucking a woman from behind,
controlling her with her heavy necklace,

a bicycle chain. The budding sapling
shook as she clung to it,

her orange dress hitched up in back.
People there throw garbage out the windows.

Who cares? Four arms, four rolled-up sleeves.

The silver slur of light along the tracks.
Four arms, four rolled-up sleeves.

The orange dress hitched up in back.

City Animals

Just before the tunnel, the train
lurches through a landscape
snatched from a dream. Flame blurts

from high up on the skeletal refinery,
all pipes and tanks. Then a tail of smoke.

The winter twilight looks like fire, too,

smeared above the bleached grasses
of the marsh, and in the shards of water

where an egret the color of newspaper
holds perfectly still, like a small angel

come to study what's wrong with the world.

In the blond reeds, a cat picks her way
from tire to oil drum,

hunting in the petrochemical stink.

Row of nipples, row of sharp ribs.
No fish in the iridescence.
Maybe a sick pigeon, or a mouse.

Across the Hudson,
Manhattan's black geometry begins to spark

as the smut of evening rises in the streets.

Somewhere in it,
a woman in fur with a plastic bag in her hand
follows a dachshund in a purple sweater,

letting him sniff a small square of dirt
studded with cigarette butts.
And in the park a scarred Doberman

drags on his choke chain toward another fight,

but his master yanks him back.
It's like the Buddhist vision of the beasts
in their temporary afterlife, each creature

locked in its own cell of misery,
the horse pulling always uphill
with its terrible load, the whip

flicking bits of skin from its back,
the cornered bear woofing with fear,

the fox's mouth red from the leg in the trap.

Animal islands, without comfort between them.
Which shall inherit the earth?

Not the interlocking kittens frozen in the trash.

Not the dog yapping itself to death
on the twentieth floor. And not the egret,
fishing in the feculent marsh

for the condom and the drowned gun.

No, the earth belongs to the spirits
that haunt the air above the sewer grates,

the dark plumes trailing the highway's
diesel moan, the multitudes
pouring from the smokestacks of the citadel

into the gaseous ocean overhead.

Where will the angel rest itself?
What map will guide it home?

from

The Snow Watcher

1998

Mistake

It was as if someone had made a mistake,
as if the child had died but her ashes
went on falling softly through her life.

A bird came and lit on a snowy branch,
a purple finch still in its summer range,

come to celebrate the first winter
of the childhood by knocking a dust of stars
into the cold, so the baby could see the miracle.

I remember a window, a green curtain,
a bird in snow, then birdless snow.

Private Airplane

On the grass airfield, a wife
is waiting in her four-wheel drive.
Soon her husband will appear
like a tiny black angel,
and when the winds and commotion

of his landing have come and gone
and I'm alone here again,
I'll carve a little memento of the evening—
a poem. As far back as I can remember,
this is how I've borne my attachment

to the world, trying to understand
what I am, scanning the sky for—what?
A god to tell me
why I'm the airplane,
and not its passenger?

Girl Riding Bareback

These late summer afternoons are so like childhood's
they take my breath and breathe it with me,
take it and breathe it without me.

Curved hot muscle of the neck, the chestnut shoulders
flowing through the uncut hay—

old August daydream come to visit
a place that looks familiar,
a field like the field it remembers—

arrows of sun falling harmless on a girl
and the big imaginary animal of her self.

Glimpse

It was as if a window suddenly blew open
and the sky outside the mind came flooding in.
My childhood shriveled to a close,

thread of smoke that rose
and touched a cloud—or the cloud's

replica adrift on the slow river of thinking—
and disappeared inside it. In that dark water,
a new lily was opening, sky-white out of the muck.

It was only a glimpse, quick,
like a bird ruffling,

but I saw the flower's
beautiful stark shape, an artichoke
brightened from within by the moon.

A path lay shadowy under my feet,
and I followed it.

Solo

Nothing to watch but the snow,
the muted road slowly unbending.
I've always been alone, and that knowledge

has been like a sheet of cold glass
between me and the world,

though it meant I could
lose myself in lonely beauties,
for example the tiny

darting fish in the headlights,
their almost wordlike scribbling.

Now that's all changed.
I am myself nothing but a quick
flake of frozen cloud,

a minnow of light that can swim
silver-bodied into the questions,

the shadowy currents
of all I long to know.
That darkness without shores.

That's what I want to be. One fish
in the numberless fish of the snow.

Animal Languages

In snow, all tracks

—animal and human—
speak to one another,

a long conversation that keeps breaking off
then starting up again.

I want to read those pages
instead of the kind
made of human words.

I want to write in the language of those
who have been to that place before me.

Secrets

All my childhood was spent
in a clubhouse for one.
Who knows the password?

I'm still afraid of the subway.
What does it mean,
the sudden telling of a secret?

There was a pure light in childhood.
It was a laser. The girl stayed in the dark,
but the pure thing burned everything.

The light again. The word *pure.*
She lay on a dishtowel. Then with the same
fingers he played the piano.

Fold up the little towel
and put it away. Fold up
the little towel, put it away.

Hologram

At the center of the iris,
there's nothing.
You can look right into
its internal darkness
as into an unlit doll's-house:

on the dining room table
a flower in a vase,
of course a tiny iris.
I'm peering in the window
of depression's house,

where I lived as a child.
It's like the inside
of an iris, twilit,
its innermost petals
closed softly over nothing.

Arsonist and Fireman

It was the hot orange edge,
the flame biting and tearing its way
out of the field—that's what I loved.

I looked up the word *loins* in the dictionary,
and lit the dry grass with its meaning.

Put that memory away now. Its magnet
is weak after all these years. It's time to stop.
He's dead, long dead, dead for years.

Let his sad soul go off by itself.
Let it rest for a while in the scorched grass.

The Innocent One

The watcher guarded the innocent one,
that was their relationship.
When the innocent one was in danger,

had angered the mother or the father
maybe, walked out on some thin ice

on purpose (for the sharp defining edges
of it) and suddenly needed a rescue,
the watcher would be the rescuer.

That allowed the innocent one to grow up
reckless: she was always stabbing herself

in the heart to see what each new kind of love
felt like. Then her savior the watcher
would heal her wound by explaining everything.

We're a very solid couple, the two of us.
We've grown up into a fine double person.

Horse

I've never seen a soul detached from its gender,
but I'd like to. I'd like to see my own that way,
free of its female tethers. Maybe it would be like
riding a horse. The rider's the human one,
but everyone looks at the horse.

Saint Animal

Suddenly it was clear to me—
I was something I hadn't been before.
It was as if the animal part of my being

had reached some maturity that gave it
authority, and had begun to use it.

I thought about death for two years.
My animal flailed and tore at its cage
till I let it go. I watched it

drift out into the easy eddies of twilight
and then veer off, not knowing me.

I'm not a bird but I'm inhabited by a spirit
that's uplifting me. It's my animal, my saint
and soldier, my flame of yearning,

come back to tell me
what it was like to be without me.

Decade

I had only one prayer, but it spread
like lilies, a single flower duplicating
itself over and over until it was rampant,

uncountable. At ten I lay dreaming
in its crushed green blades.

How did I come by it, strange notion
that the hard stems of rage could be broken,
that the lilies were made of words,

my words? Each one I picked
laid a wish to rest. I mean killed it.

The difference between prayer
and a wish is that a wish knows it will be
a failure even as it sets out,

whereas a prayer is still innocent.
Wishing wants prayer to find that out.

Erotic Energy

Don't tell me we're not like plants,
sending out a shoot when we need to,
or spikes, poisonous oils, or flowers.

Come to me but only when I say,
that's how plants announce

the rules of propagation.
Even children know this. You can
see them imitating all the moves

with their bright plastic toys.
So that, years later, at the moment

the girl's body finally says yes
to the end of childhood,
a green pail with an orange shovel

will appear in her mind like a tropical
blossom she has never seen before.

A Last Look Back

Things change behind my back.
The starting snow I was just watching
has escaped into the past.

Well, not the past, but the part of the world
that surrounds the moment at hand.

That's why, whenever I see
animal tracks in a light snow like this,
I think of footnotes.

So strange, to inhabit a space
and then leave it vacant, standing open.

Each change in me is a stone step
beneath the blur of snow.
In spring the sharp edges cut through.

When I look back, I see my former selves,
numerous as the trees.

Makeshifts

Nothing has a name it can't
slip out of. The waterfall is solid ice
by late November; the white pines
vanish under snow that's
blue in the morning, pink in the dusk.

Here's a little bouquet—ice
and evergreen and sun, three moments
arranged for human looking,
though it's only the husks of their names
that I've gathered and paralyzed.

Paint

Lotions and scents, ripe figs,
raw silk, the cat's striped pelt…
Fat marbles the universe.

I want to be a faint pencil line
under the important words,
the ones that tell the truth.

Delicious, the animal trace
of the brush in the paint,
crushed caviar of molecules.

A shadow comes to me and says,
When you go, please leave
the leafless branch unlocked.

I paint the goat's yellow eye,
and the latch on truth's door.
Open, eye and door.

Hunger for Something

Sometimes I long to be the woodpile,
cut-apart trees soon to be smoke,
or even the smoke itself,

sinewy ghost of ash and air, going
wherever I want to, at least for a while.

Neither inside nor out,
neither lost nor home, no longer
a shape or a name, I'd pass through

all the broken windows of the world.
It's not a wish for consciousness to end.

It's not the appetite an army has
for its own emptying heart,
but a hunger to stand now and then

alone on the death-grounds,
where the dogs of the self are feeding.

My Taste for Trash

I've got a taste for trashy thrillers,
their psychological sex and violence,
sometimes two in a night.

They're like heavy velvet curtains:
no stray light spoils the darkness,

no sound of the world comes through.
The real is elsewhere.
The real guns, cold to the touch.

The real boys, their eyes opaque,
no longer human.

And when they die,
they turn to stars in the star-clogged night.
This is a tale you could tell

any place on earth, in any century,
and people would already know it.

To the Reader:
The Language of the Cloud

Come with me to a private room.
I have a secret to show you.
Sometimes I like to stand outside it

with a stranger because I haven't
come at it from that vantage in so long—

see? There I am beside him, still joined,
still kissing. Isn't it dreamlike,
the way the bed drifts in its dishevelment?

Bereft of their clothes, two humans
lie entangled in its cloud.

Their bodies are saying the after-grace,
still dreaming in the language of the cloud.
Look at them, neither two nor one.

I want them to tell me what they know
before the amnesia takes them.

Today's Lapses

There's a country I like to visit.
We're like a man and his mistress—
I'm not going to marry it, not going to give it up.

I visit all three of its provinces.
Their names are Anger, Ignorance, and Greed.

When I cross the line between embellishment
and a lie, there's a warning ache,
but also a scrap of color where none was.

Tomorrow, I'll spend some time pondering
the kinship of the color and the ache.

No zazen today. I've strayed off
on my own beyond the pasture's edge,
where the lupine's in full bloom.

Summer has just finished opening.
Don't look for me tonight.

Stray

The cat was starving, missing a foreleg,
and winter right next door.
A neighbor killed its pain with one shot.

My mind follows the delicate three-blossom tracks
across snow.

It won't leave the cat alone,
circling and circling the stiffening body
already claimed by the snow—

and I, the observer, follow it
as if I held its long unbreakable leash.

Look at the wind, invisible river,
look at the breaking mirror of the brook.
Is this the place where thoughts arise and vanish?

Which part is the cat
and which the mind?

To the Reader:
Polaroids

Who are you, austere little cloud
drawn to this page, this sky in the dream
I'm having of meeting you here?

There should be a word that means "tiny sky."
Probably there is, in Japanese.
A verbal Polaroid of a Polaroid.

But you're the sky, not a cloud.
I'm the cloud. I gather and dissipate,
but you are always here.

Leave a message for me if you can.
Break a twig on the lilac, or toss
a few dried petals on the hood of my car.

May neither of us forsake the other.
The cloud persists in the darkness,
but the darkness does not persist.

Architecture

I peer into Japanese characters
as into faraway buildings
cut from the mind's trees.

In the late afternoon a small bird
shakes a branch, lets drop a white splash.

In the wind, in the rain,
the delicate wire cage glistens,
empty of suet.

Poetry's not window-cleaning.
It breaks the glass.

To the Reader:
If You Asked Me

I want you with me, and yet you are the end
of my privacy. Do you see how these rooms
have become public? How we glance to see if—
who? Whom did you imagine?
Surely we're not here alone, you and I.

I've been wandering
where the cold tracks of language
collapse into cinders, unburnable trash.
Beyond that, all I can see is the remote cold
of meteors before their avalanches of farewell.

If you asked me what words
a voice like this one says in parting,
I'd say, *I'm sweeping an empty factory*
toward which I feel neither hostility nor nostalgia.
I'm just a broom, sweeping.

To the Reader:
Twilight

Whenever I look
out at the snowy
mountains at this hour
and speak directly
into the ear of the sky,
it's you I'm thinking of.
You're like the spirits
the children invent
to inhabit the stuffed horse
and the doll.
I don't know who hears me.
I don't know who speaks
when the horse speaks.

from

Dog Language

2005

Skeleton

No one dead will ever
read these words,
and those alive now
will sweep them from the streets.
The writing of our time most
likely to survive is graffiti.
It survives war.
So why not spray letters
you can see a long way off,
"the plain picture,"
as Bob Dylan put it.
"Truth…," he said, "why,
Truth is just the plain picture."

The dogs run through half-thawed
woods, barking the holy scary
words rote in a child,
ruins and crosses and bones,
never outgrown.
And they dig at the gray roses
of hives collapsed in snow,
nothing but paper, words
saying there was honey once.

I asked Truth what to worship,
and Truth said Death,
looking up from licking
the caviar of moments

from Death's hand.
So here are the bones
in the exploded view,
pelvis and vertebrae,
thrown dice of hands.
Look at the skull.
I'm its voice.

The Paper River

The most beloved body
of my childhood was Johns Brook,
its bed of ancient broken pears,
icy libations pouring
over them for centuries.
Through the leaky oval mask
I entered its alcoves and grand halls,
its precincts of green-brown light,
the light of my infant thinking.
In the minnow-bright roar
I saw the place where life and art
meet under water, stone to stone,
with the sunken treasure and trash.
The sound of the brook
was the sound of the house,
the pools of the kitchen and bedrooms.
A galaxy away it would still be
the background of my sleep.

Clouds came down to earth,
great gloomy rooms among the trees,
dark rooms of the brook,
church of deep pools.
As soon as you entered
you were wholly alone in it,
all sinewy ladders
and gray stairs, stones magnified,
and the sidelong trout,

all gone now,
rainbows and brookies,
one big one per pool,
gills like fresh cuts.

I dove into the flume's mystery,
no place you could touch bottom
or see all the way down in
because half at least
was always in shadow.
It was like learning a room
by carrying a candle
corner to corner,
looking for God to see if He, too,
were awake and listening
to the river crumpling and erasing,
enforcing its laws.
I found a cold, an oblique god,
who commanded me to answer
all my questions by myself.

The English language
is also a beautiful river,
full of driftwood and detritus,
bones hung with trinkets,
scant beaches more stones than sand.
And up on the hills it's the wind
touching the juniper spurned
by the cows, its thistle sharpness,
and the fawn's hoof
left by coyotes,
in their scat.

Dangerous Playgrounds

The father is teaching his eight-year-old
to clean a grouse, the purple-gray skin
pimpled by plucking,
and so delicate that one roughly pulled
pinch of feathers could tear it,
with little bruises where
the shot went in.
If you push on the bumpy
sole of a foot, the toes
wrap around your finger
like a baby's hand. It's a reflex.
He says *clean,* not *gut*
as the other fathers do,
the organs slippery and ruby,
nothing soft, even the liver
rubbery, and the heart,
hard as an unripe cherry,
all of it smelling
like neither excrement nor sex,
but something in between.

At the piano, someone's great-uncle
entertained the children in the uninsulated
octagonal room, clean Yankee architecture
a century old. We sang "Auld Lang Syne"
and *I have ridden the wind,*
I have ridden the sea,
I have ridden the ghosts that flee
from the vaults of death

with a chilling breath
over all of Galilee.
I already knew that words
do not live entirely inside language.
No one told me;
I could see exactly where the breaches were,
the place we're supposed to turn around
and go back. Beyond that was the sting,
electric fence, and beyond that
a feather caught in a twig,
strange graft,
and I made a note to myself:
don't ignore this,
thus inviting the sting.

I often think about the doll's house
in *The Tale of Two Bad Mice*
by Beatrix Potter.
While the two dolls were out,
Tom Thumb and his wife-mouse
Hunca Munca briefly set up housekeeping
there, though it was a disappointment—
the miniature plaster foods inedible,
the lead knife bending on the painted ham,
nothing real, nothing as they expected.
In their disillusionment
they vandalized the place,
smashing the lobster glued to its plate,
jamming the fake fish into the fake fire.
It was a scene of seduction and abandonment,
the riches glimmering all around them,
and then the joke.

A Lamb by Its Ma

Just before it rains, the lilacs
thrash weakly,
storm-light heightening
the clusters drooping
at their peak of scent,
wind running
through them like slow water,
then a splash, mood swing:
leaves spangled with drops
from inside the storm.
Mary made us come inside
if there was lightning,
flapping a white towel
to call us back.
We hung around the kitchen
drinking tea till it cleared.
She brought us tea at bedtime.
A good cup of black tea
and you'll sleep like a lamb by its ma.
She told us that our parents
loved us, that their war
was theirs alone.
She said it in the charged air,
in the scent of their absence
from the house,
their clean absence.
If thunder came at night,
she told about the brave

and faithful dogs of Scotland,
how a shepherd knows
where his lamb has gone
by bits of wool in the wire.

Cocktail Music

All my life a brook of voices
has run in my ears,
many separate instruments
tuning and playing, tuning.
It's cocktail music,
the sound of my parents
in their thirties,
glass-lined ice bucket loaded
and reloaded but no one tending bar,
little paper napkins, cigarettes,
kids passing hors d'oeuvres.
It's drinking music,
riffle of water over stones,
ice in glasses, rise and fall
of many voices touching—
that music. Husbands grilling meat,
squirting the fire to keep it down,
a joke erupting, bird voices snipping
at something secret by the bar.
It's all the voices collapsed
into one voice,
urgent and muscled like a river
then lowered as in a drought,
but never gone. It's the background.
When I lift the shell to my ear
it's in there.

Auld Lang Syne

Perfume of snow
melting in the hall,
on the slates.
Dull with old smoke,
the eyes of the moose preside;
his antlers uphold
someone's wet gloves.
He has a bald spot on his neck
where people stroke him for luck,
and a wreath of balsam.
At fifteen I touched the place
where the world touched him.
Fly back, wild flocks of the senses,
eavesdrop at the shrines
of the fireplace and bar.
Bring something back:
live coal of lipstick
or some resinous
perfume for the New Year.

Summers, we'd steal out onto
the golf course of the private club
to make love under the Perseid showers,
soaked by the wet velvet green.
They were just boys,
but we longed for them
and lay with them.

Who would refuse such an imprint?
I wear it still like a string of cold beads.

There's a virgin sadness trapped
in the old house, museum of summer,
furnace cranked up for Christmas.
The adults stir their cocktails with icicles.
The kids kiss in the halls.
Four generations of match-strikes
stripe the blackened hearth.
The fire-eyes of the andiron owls
are watching the men, who have
wrapped the dog in a towel.
Mrs. M's bleared mouth
repeats that *quills*
are hydraulic—cut off the tips
and they'll come right out,
which turns out to be untrue.
They use pliers, and afterward
the dog wags in apology
and the drinking resumes.

Marijuana

Stoned by noon, I'd take the trail
that runs along the X River
in the State of Y, summer of '69,
crows' black ruckus overhead.
I'd wade through the ferns' sound
of vanishing to the almost-invisible ledge,
stark basin canted out to the southwest:
sheltered, good drainage,
full sun, remote, state land.
You could smell the blacker, foreign green
from a long way off when it rained,
incense-grade floral, the ripening spoils,
then pang of wood smoke,
antiseptic pitch and balsam,
scents cut like initials into a beech,
then cold that kills the world for a while,
puts it under, then wakes it up
again in spring when it's still tired.
I woke from its anesthetic
wanting the tight buds of my loneliness
to swell and split, not die in waiting.
It was why I rushed through everything,
why I tore away at the perpetual gauze
between me and the stinging world,
its starlight and resins,
new muscle married to smoke and tar,
just wedding the world for a while.

About to divorce it, too,
to marry some other smoke and tar.

On snowshoes in falling snow,
we lugged peat, manure,
and greensand a mile up there.
Alfalfa meal, spent hops.
The clones bronzed, hairy and sticky,
and a week before frost we'd slice
the dirt around them with a bread knife,
which gave the dope
a little extra turpentine.
Weed, reefer, smoke—
It was one of life's perfumes.
Sometimes its flower opens
on a city street, gray petals,
phantom musk dispersing.

Sleeping out on the high ledges
on a bed of blueberries dwarfed
by wind and springy beneath the blankets,
we'd watch for meteors and talk till dawn,
gazing toward the pinnacle in the distance,
pyramid to the everlasting glory
of Never Enough, not far below us
in his tomb, asleep in the granite chill
with the bones of his faithful animals.

Could this be the pinnacle?
To be slumming back there,
buoyant on the same old
wave just breaking,

now the wave of words, the liftoff?
I'm still cracking open the robin's egg
to see the yellow heart, the glue.
A pinnacle is a fulcrum,
a scale. And now that it's tipped
I can look back through the ghost
of self-consciousness to its embryo,
first the tomboy,
then the chick in a deerskin skirt,
the first breaking of the spirit,
the heart's deflowerment.

Caw, caw, a crow wants to peck
at the ember of the mind
as it was before it tasted
the dark meat of the world.
But I can call it back—
the match's sulfur spurt,
its petals of carbon and tar,
a flash of mind, a memory:
how after each deflowerment
I became the flower.

Bonsai

What's pornographic about them
is the intimacy with which one
can regard the other: the one
made to be displayed—
five berries, red, helpless at the hands,
the fingers and scissors of the other,
while the other can scrutinize
from any angle whenever it wants.
That's the obscenity.

Listen, former self:
you're a child.
I no longer have a child in me.
I feel my bones in the handrail,
tree skeleton, hardwood
that remembers how the human
got into its body,
the tree into the little tree.
I'm no one's mother now.
I abandon you here.
I'll speak of you no more.

Soul in Space

How did it come to be
that a particular human loneliness
set forth into clouds of ignorance
so as to more closely examine itself?
Why one and so few others?

I stand among shoulder-high canes,
looking directly into their barbed
inner dark to the snake, or caterpillar—
actually a handful of blackberries
in the green shade, reptilian
yet warm, momentarily still.

I want my obituary to say that
I wrote in the language of dogs
and not that I sat sprinkling
black letters on a white ladder,
leading my own eye down
one rung at a time
until the dog was gone.

New England Slate Pane

Mom has already made arrangements
for a spot inside the churchyard wall
among the old Yankee slates,
some fallen, and the granites
from foreign places,
tilted by frost.
A mason sets them straight
again each spring.
Perennials for the formal beds
accepted with gratitude;
no other plantings allowed.
Cut flowers may be laid on the graves.
Someone might leave
plastic tulips as a joke.
Otherwise, silence, nothing,
trees living their interior lives,
visitors wandering
among the oldest stones.
This is where she wants to lie,
next to wind-pruned beach roses,
paths of crushed shells.

Somebody finally bought that farm
and orchard I like to drive past
at blossom time,
mud runnels in the roads,
trees way past mature.
For ten years no one's come

to prune or feed or mow the aisles.
Bare scatterings of flowers
alight on broken branches.
Who let it all go?
What broke in the family?

Now the elderly apples will spend
their twilight in the paintings of a man
who bought them
in order to study their end.
She wants her marker spare like that,
just name and dates.
Time's black-and-white bouquet.

Cities of Mind

From up here on the parapets
I can see skeletons of meaning strewn
among stones, all the way east
to childhood's shaded rooms.
To the west lie the cities
I've not yet imagined,
and those I never will.

Let's admit it's an addiction,
this scribbling-turned-typing.
How else might we speak of it?
As an anxiety? In any case,
I seem to like its fangs in my heart.

On Dad's eightieth birthday
we had a little party
in the "Living Room,"
the whole herd of wheelchairs
drawn like magnets to the smell of cake,
the snuffed-out candles.

I'm sorry my father keeps barging in here.
He usually doesn't stay very long.
He's an old man who was once a man.
And one of Mom's shadows falls
from time to time, just so you know.

Jim Richardson says, "All work
is the avoidance of harder work"—
true in my case. When the carpenters
started on the porch, I moved
the computer to the guest room,
where I had to crawl under the bed
with an extension cord to get juice.
Then I had to fight hedges
of castoffs, wrapping papers and ribbons,
a plastic serpent's nest of
strapping tape unwilling
to stay in the wastebasket,
the snake's name something like
anaconda, boa constrictor, python,
rattler... oh, I know: *time consumer.*

Confetti, glitter, glamour,
the frosting flowers and the hopeless
little figurines glued to the cake—
what happens to those?
Do people save them?
Pass them down the generations?

When Nan got into coyote bait,
I drove her through the wee hours
to the fancy animal hospital far away,
thinking, *Let her live, let her not suffer,*
then, *Let her die quickly,*
thus killing the snake of my fear
along with the dog.

See what happens if you leave
the blossoms on the tree?
They go on blooming,
obscuring the thorns,
and before you know it
a scarf of identity has distracted you,
a jewel of history glinted in your eye...

Raised on the classic myths,
I see the drift nets of latitude
and longitude on the night sky
inhabited by beasts and gods.
On Pegasus I fled the hunter,
the centaur, the satyr,
riding the star-horse out to free
the greater and lesser bears,
the major and minor dogs,
caged in their constellations.

Tech Help

My bonsai teacher says to *quit doing it like a girl.*
I'm pruning the root-ball of a *Podocarpus,*
or Buddhist pine, trained semicascade.

The first time Dad fell,
the femur broke in eleven places
due to his artificial knee (titanium and steel).
A rod screwed to the bones in thirteen places
didn't work, and the graft stayed weak.
For two years he fought his wheelchair
into near submission. The grand finale
was his riding it down two flights of stairs
without tipping over or falling out.
The nurses loved him.

The last time I called tech help
I got George in Salt Lake, at work
at six in the morning their time.
He was very helpful.
I offered to write a note for his file,
but he said, *It's okay, Chase.*
Your compliment is enough.

Arcade

I write for the euphoria
of thunderstorms,
gravity and uplift at once,
and the jing-jing-jing of luck
in the arcade's private rooms.
I play here every day
in the maze of thinking,
of music and weeping and visions:
someone cracking ice in the kitchen,
a ghost in a silver chair.
Where else can I
find the half-human girl
with dog blood in her veins,
or crash again at the condemned hotel,
empty after the auction,
in which our pack met and coupled,
talked and smoked pot
until the fire department persuaded
the owners to let them burn it
so the men could practice
on controlled fire?

In Japan, pachinko's everywhere.
What a beautiful toy the boys have,
the parlors, palaces of ardor and cash.
They live as in an ant farm
built of frosted glass.
You can see them mating

with the wife-body machines,
the cash flow of each courtship,
which might go on flowing
and ebbing for days, until
a senior male relative or friend
drags the addict home.

In my favorite video blackjack game,
two disembodied, white-gloved hands
shoot their cuffs,
snap and flex the deck
with slight impatience: *Your bet?*
The chip-clink's ultrarealistic
on the cyberfelt, dollar a bet.
Phantom Belle, that's my machine.

The Ceiling

I'm conscious of my bones
where they touch the porcelain.
The tub stays cold beneath
the water's heat,
so it's the two colds that
recognize each other here
in this grotto of earthly delights,
candles enlivening
the tile overhead,
the perfumed foam
I lie beneath.

A word alighting
on the tongue-tip,
then gone again…
And my eyes are changing.
Oh, the fussing over glasses.
The mind sees its own machines
blacken and break down,
beaten back into the earth
near the railroad bed:
wire carts, sodden nests
beneath the overpass.
Who sleeps there,
among the dead umbrellas?

Uh-oh, I'm lying here glistening
and warm in the river Styx

thinking of death again,
bones in a catacomb.
A trickle keeps it hot,
but the suds are gone.
Look at my fifty-two-year-old legs,
starting to ache
for their last lover, the dirt.

Cinderblock

On the first warm day,
the aides fret about his pate,
fetch his hat. I push him
out the automatic doors
into the pallid sun.
Dad thinks we should
stay put until all the Indians
are back in their tepees,
but right now he's off to teach
a Latin class. Where are his keys?
They're a few miles away,
in the past, where he's no longer
active in the community.
I steer him along the asphalt
paths of the grounds: bark mulch,
first green shoots,
puddle of coffee by a car.
I loop around so he can discover
the pile of construction materials twice,
the word *cinderblock* coming to him
more quickly the second time.

Verizon

My father had been "climbing,"
so they moved him down
toward the nurses' station;
very confusing: first a new room
and now his telephone is dead.
He repeats the word *Verizon*
at the speed of a slow hammock
while I call Repair on my cell.
This is not how it's meant to be,
the wire serpent recoiling
from him as if to strike
at his memory, his recovery,
lithe black spiral,
strong willed, heavy dial tone
swinging upside down. Sometimes
when he pushes the luminous buttons
a woman tells him all about Verizon,
using the word in many beautiful sentences,
spreading it out for him like a golf course
on which he looks forward to playing,
but sometimes he answers her rudely,
manhandling the receiver,
cursing Verizon and his outlaw hands.
Or he's pissed because the aide
brings him the telephone, saying,
It's your daughter isn't that nice?
as if it were any business of hers.
You couldn't film this. No one

would be able to bear it,
skeletons everywhere,
riding around on silver wheels,
pure oxygen piped straight to skulls
crowned by near-colorless
chains of proteins, the hair.
I saw not just my father's
long bones but also the knowledge
they withhold from him,
catheter, sponge bath,
titanium and steel.
Oh hell, the tea's cold.
Verizon, izon, izon, zon.
Birds of cyberspace sing in his ear,
bright notes and numbers, urging him
to *Visit our website to find out more.*

My Listener

When hope forms a bud of prayer,
who picks it?
Words in all languages
yearn toward the stars,
confessing and beseeching.

I talk to a masculine higher power
half god, half human.
When he sits calm and golden,
spine straight as the Buddha's,
my own spine yearns upward
toward the clean sky of his face.
But when he lounges
on the butcher's throne,
setting wars on fire from afar
then hunting in the gutted,
rotting lands, he's my enemy, the one
who lifted my father from the cradle
in his claws so many years ago,
then let him fall,
a stick of driftwood someone saved,
provenance unknown.

Dad waits for cocktail hour,
cookies and juice,
repeating the words *voice mail* to himself,
anxious about the new technologies,
the fax and the microwave.

At night in his stainless crib
he addresses
the One Who Knows Everything
Yet Does Nothing, who ekes out
a bright fistful of candies
to keep the game alive
while the child prays for death,
shaking the safety rails.

When my Listener shows me his ribs,
all my austerities gather around me,
earnest and gray, and I vow
to make myself invisible,
possessionless,
a servant of the world.
But he's only a demigod,
and jealous. He commands me
to meet him in private.
I tell him the truth insofar
as I know it. He says nothing.
We always meet in private.
When he whips his starving flocks
I'm there alone with him.

Dog Biscuits

After my father's cremation,
my sisters and I agreed
to bury him privately
when the ground thawed.
One will plant a flowering tree,
one see to the stone and its cutting,
one call the gravedigger and the town clerk.
It'll be just us, the daughters,
presiding over ashes that could be
any mammal's, or those of any love
dispersible by wind.

Let's bury the secret violence to his dogs,
Pompey and Tara, Juba and Molly,
their ashes already gone to this ground.
And his "escapades," as Mom called them.
Here withers that branch of the tree.

Let's bury the ring inscribed
In perpetuum ave atque vale (translated
"Hail and farewell" by my father,
"Hello, and goodbye forever" by Mom,
a token dating back to the First Separation)
and a tennis ball for canine shades.
Your dad is with his dogs now,
said more than one person at the funeral.

It'll be just us, the three inheritors,
on a raw windy day in Death's kingdom,
lifting our eyes from the hole
to the mountains hazed with spring,
saying, *In perpetuum ave atque vale,*
minor god of our father.
Let's each of us drop a few
dog biscuits into his grave.

Vestibule

What etiquette holds us back
from more intimate speech,
especially now, at the end of the world?
Can't we begin a conversation
here in the vestibule,
then gradually move it inside?
What holds us back
from saying things outright?
We've killed the earth.
Yet we speak of other things.
Our words should cauterize
all wounds to the truth.

A Negative of Snow

Though many moonless nights
have fallen on the grave
like a negative of snow,
Dad's wheelchair sometimes
flashes in my mind, and I hear
the bleating down the hall,
a voice berating its god,
his worthless anodynes,
and the doctors who were
at that very moment
increasing his morphine,
having failed to note
the word *alcoholic* on his chart,
meaning that his damaged liver
routed the opiates straight
to his brain, his beautiful fragile brain,
which I had not yet finished loving.
My father, who still had manners,
who was a hardwood, a tough tree.
That was his first death.

Monastery Nights

I like to think about the monastery
as I'm falling asleep, so that it comes
and goes in my mind like a screen saver.
I conjure the lake of the zendo,
rows of dark boats still unless
someone coughs or otherwise
ripples the calm.
I can hear the four a.m. slipperiness
of sleeping bags as people turn over
in their bunks. The ancient bells.

When I was first falling in love with Zen,
I burned incense called *Kyo-nishiki*,
"Kyoto Autumn Leaves,"
made by the Shoyeido Incense Company,
Kyoto, Japan. To me it smelled like
earnestness and ether, and I tried to imagine
a consciousness ignorant of me.
I just now lit a stick of it. I had to run downstairs
for some rice to hold it upright in its bowl,
which had been empty for a while,
a raku bowl with two fingerprints
in the clay. It calls up the monastery gate,
the massive door demanding I recommit myself
in the moments of both its opening
and its closing, its weight now mine.
I wanted to know what I was,

and thought I could find the truth
where the floor hurts the knee.

I understand no one I consider to be religious.
I have no idea what's meant when someone says
they've been intimate with a higher power.
I seem to have been born without a god receptor.
I have fervor but seem to lack
even the basic instincts of the many seekers,
mostly men, I knew in the monastery,
sitting zazen all night,
wearing their robes to near-rags
boy-stitched back together with unmatched thread,
smoothed over their laps and tucked under,
unmoving in the long silence,
the field of grain ripening, heavy tasseled,
field of sentient beings turned toward candles,
flowers, the Buddha gleaming
like a vivid little sports car from his niche.

What is the mind that precedes
any sense we could possibly have
of ourselves, the mind of self-ignorance?
I thought that the divestiture of self
could be likened to the divestiture
of words, but I was wrong.
It's not the same work.
One's a transparency
and one's an emptiness.

Kyo-nishiki...
Today I'm painting what Mom

calls no-colors, grays and browns,
evergreens: what's left of the woods
when autumn's come and gone.
And though he died, Dad's here,
still forgetting he's no longer
married to Annie,
that his own mother is dead,
that he no longer owns a car.

Surprise half inch of snow.
What good are words?

And what about birches in moonlight,
Russell handing me the year's
first chanterelle—
Shouldn't God feel like that?

I aspire to "a self-forgetful,
perfectly useless concentration,"
as Elizabeth Bishop put it.
So who shall I say I am?
I'm a prism, an expressive temporary
sentience, a pinecone falling.
I can hear my teacher saying, *No.*
That misses it.
Buddha goes on sitting through the century,
leaving me alone in the front hall,
which has just been cleaned and smells of pine.

Work Libido

The year I turned fourteen,
Grandma taught me five-card stud
and took my allowance for the week.
In casinos I usually play blackjack.
I like the speed and scale,
companion strangers fingering their chips,
and the background ruckus of slots
and cybersounds, coins
cascading into man-sized Dixie cups.

Each sentience is brief, is it not?
Therefore I'm trying to record whatever
I can of the instantly squandered present
so I can say in stone-plain words
what sentience is.

Rules: *Tell the truth. No decoration. Remember death.*

As far as I can tell, there's no
such thing as a "present moment."
To me they're like atoms:
faster than imagination,
intermarried, unto themselves,
their boundaries invisible
and their numbers unknown.
I think of them as paint rather
than as words, though of course
the two smear where they overlap.

Gamblers and poets share
a passion for what's next: the flush
disguised as a boat with a hole
(that's poker talk), or a rift
in the poem, a soft spot that yields
the sticky perfume of pine pitch,
like burned honey but resinous,
spicy, antiseptic, a conduit straight
to childhood with its ferns
incompletely unfurled,
their not-quite-mature spores
glistening like caviar among green feathers.
And to the little diamond snake that slithered
round my neck (but only for a while).

Sorry, I'm quite distracted.
A breeze from the next poem
has slipped into this one,
so my mind is playing with
the sound of reptilian fountains
and the racing colors of the chips,
the clay and composite resins
always cool to the touch.
The playground is empty,
and from here the casino sounds
like an ocean of tiny bells.

Thought Satellite

What a strange world this is,
dime-sized Earth in the background
of Death's portrait in the dining room.
It spins on, its nations charred,
its altars still on fire,
its playgrounds still.

I think of poems as a series
of small harsh rebirths—
I keep passing myself in the halls
of a house where every room
has a second door,
so I never have to go out
the way I came in.

It's quitting time. The carpenters
working on the porch left at four,
and the dogs need a run.
So goodbye; I'm dying out
of this communion now,
into the next rebirth:
an August afternoon at the pinnacle,
scent of balsam spiked by rain,
the field glittering.

Somebody's chain saw
barks at the afternoon.

Andy Gates is flying
his Cessna all over the valley,
looking for his girlfriend's car.

Well, that's it. See you.

Horses Where the Answers Should Have Been

New Poems

Snow-globe of Vesuvius

I live on the flank of Vesuvius, in Pompeii.
Each day the sky fills with leaflets,
smokelets, prayers to powers
aglitter whether storming or still
(the old ones mica,
the new ones who-cares-what).

Everyone knows there's more than one
kind of consciousness. Everyone knows
that in the snow-globe of Vesuvius,
the "snow" is really ash—
each time, the volcano buries the town.

Would you meet me in a world like that?
If not there, where?

The Long Bony Faces of the Mules

In an early memory, the heads
of two black mules appear out of fog
over a single strand of barbed wire.
In another I stand rattling the crib bar,
alone, my bottle on the floor.
Who threw it? And what was held up
to the long bony faces of the mules?

Why do I desire to see things
as they are without me,
or claim as my ancestor
the mountain hermit in a cave
with no distractions, no companion minds?
I don't know. Who wants to know?

Back in the days when a child could
ride her bike two miles to school
on the first warm morning, sweater arms
around her waist, the infant leaves
unlocked at last, and not think
about anything but words for the hard tires
striping the litter of fallen buds, wholly
absorbed by the spoilage and mystery,
I knew nothing of the fences words make
in the mind, or that I would devote
the first half of my life to building them
and the second to tearing them down.

Tourist Traps

It's Upstate New York in the 1950s,
land of amusements,
natural wonders like Ausable Chasm
and High Falls Gorge,
and tourist traps, kiddie parks
like Land of Makebelieve,
a castle with a dungeon, and train cars
just wide enough for one kid.
You can still see pink turrets through the trees,
and under the eaves the paper lanterns of wasps.

At 1,000 Animals you could drive a cart
pulled by an ostrich, or pose for a Polaroid
with a boa at the Serpentarium,
then feed him a mouse. Or watch
boys in a pit milk snakes for venom.

Nothing's left but Santa's Workshop,
June through August. Frontier Town's gone.
The antique stagecoach
jounced on a flatbed out of town.

When I can't sleep or am trying to stay
awake in the car, I slip back
into the traffic of children roaming
the child-sized streets, floating
past their parents on the carousel.
I hand-feed the deer.

I walk in and out of the fake jail,
and climb the castle's stucco tower.

I don't stay too long.
I don't want to end up
trapped in a place where
childhood never ends.

Math Trauma

If you liked geometry,
it meant you were a prude.
Girls who liked algebra put out.
The cool girls (I was not one)
sat cloistered, passing notes
and scoring high on tests.

The first time Mom and Dad split up,
kids from down the block and I lit the dry field
behind the development, then with wet towels
beat back the racing edge on the verge of panic
until we were sure it was out.
I always got that feeling from math.

I writhed like a snake over coals
if it came near me.
Mrs. X, drunk the year we did
multiplication and division,
never checked our workbooks
so no one ever saw the horses
where the answers should have been.
That's when I first wandered off into
the white pastures on my own,
with nothing but a spiky quiver of words
and an urgent question.

Tomboyhood

My father bought me this because
I begged him; he was getting shotgun
shells, going bird hunting;
I wanted to be his son.
It's a Buck knife with a belt-loop sheath
and a whetstone. I keep it on my desk,
memento mori of that strange
between-age for girls,
not-yet-ended and not-yet-begun.

Aren't memories just
dreams of consciousness,
clouds snagged in a tree?
To remember is to choose among dreams,
though sometimes a dream chooses first.

Hoping to win the Shetland pony
or the pup tent, kids sold seeds
door-to-door, letting ladies
riffle the packets in the cardboard display.
Sometimes we'd ring the bell and then hide.
I hid with a man in a tent of leaves.
Is there a dead child inside?
No, it's a dog with her head rolled back,
mouth frozen open, wrapped in a tarp.
Not my dog. I don't know the dog.
I bury her where no one will ever find her.

Savin Rock

What I know is a slur of memory,
fantasy, research, pure invention,
crime dramas, news, and witnesses
like the girl who liked to get high
and the one who was eventually
returned to her family unharmed.
The rest I made up.

The fathers drank beer in the grandstand,
flattening cans and dropping
the dull coins into the underworld.
It was daylight—we went right under,
down into the slatted dark,
the smell under the bleachers
where lots of men peed,
paper cones and dead balloons,
people jostling and whispering.
Down there were the entrances
to the dark rides, the funhouses:
Death Valley and Laff-in-the-Dark.
Of course that's not true;
they were right on the main boardwalk
under strings of bulbs lit up all night.

Mom says, *To remember something,*
go back to the place where you forgot it.
But the place was torn down
forty years ago; there are motels

there now, where the Ferris wheel
lurched up and over the trees,
over the fathers at their picnic table
close enough to feel the Tilt-A-Whirl's
crude rhythms through the ground.
They make the cars go faster or slower, depending.
After hours the boys loosen up the machines
and take girls for rides.

Hey kid! I flipped a coin in my head
and it came up tails. Want to take a walk?
He looked older than our parents.
How old did our parents look?
He was fifty, or thirty. I remember
the smell of whatever he put on his hair,
and the blue nail on his thumb.
He could flip a lit cigarette around
with his lips so the fire was inside.
I rode a little metal car
into Laff-in-the-Dark to dance
with the skeleton (possibly real
since some teeth had fillings)
that flung itself at me from the dark.

A dog watched me from a pickup window.
The World's Biggest Pig lay
beached on its side, heaving.
The tattooed lady had a tattooed baby.
No one ever tattooed a newborn child
for real, did they? The Chinese Dragon
was only an iguana.
The go-kart man asked me if I wanted

a little on the side. I said no.
His friend in the bleachers
blew me a kiss.
In the Maze of Mirrors
I was fatso and skeleton,
skirt blown up by a fan. Not true.
A fan blew a girl's skirt up.
It wasn't me. I was a tomboy. I wore pants.

At the stable, girls in love with horses
visited and groomed and fed them daily.
For girls it was about trust,
being part of a couple,
the horse and the girl,
but for the man in the barn
it was about making girls feel
groomed and visited.
Come on over here. Didn't a guy ever
brush your hair with a currycomb?
I don't believe it! Not once?
Little honeycomb like you?
And kittens, always good bait.
A little dish of spoiled milk.
Do you think they don't pass them around?
They pass them around.
Marked kids get shared,
little pink kid tongues *lick lick licking*
like a puppy! Good dog!
And on the carousel a man appeared
from nowhere to help her on,
hand palm up on the saddle just as she sat,

squirming there until the horse pulled her away.
Little cowgirl, giddy-up!

Thus she became half human half animal,
and remained so her entire life,
now a shepherdess, now a sleek young
she-goat, so lithe and small-hipped,
half tame, little goatskin haunches—
hand-fed on snow cones and cotton candy—
the girl who was eventually
returned to her family unharmed.

Tell me, little shepherdess,
how this bodes for first love:
the centaur pissing outside your tent
in the afterlife, having come down
over the stony pastures to claim you
and feed you trout and fiddleheads
and take you to bed on the high ledges
where the wind holds you down for him.
But he won't be the first.

Sweet-sharp bouquet of darkroom,
holster with toy six-gun,
hot umbrella lamps nudged into place
by his fat pink fingers.
A little maraschino light presides over
negatives strung up like game to dry.
The tomboy's showing her rump,
hard little buttocks under the tender wrapping,
the skin. Little wonton.

Walky-talky

Sometimes in early evening neighborhood kids
played in the unfinished house,
or sat in the saddle-seat of the front loader
ditched on the future lawn.
We were children; we went where we wanted,
skirting the backyards under the salt of stars.
If you stuck a flashlight in your mouth
you could see the blood inside the cheeks,
but not the bones. Two tin cans and a taut string
made a telephone through which a voice
could be heard but not understood.
Walky-talkies sputtered and failed.
To whom did I imagine I was speaking?
Someone invisible in the airwaves,
hidden in the infinite leaves of June.

How strange, to send out words,
like fishing without a hook,
just a glittering lure cast into space
baited with some morsel of kid-consciousness,
who knows what now, probably
the wish for a horse, or a spell
to ward off the alcoholic tang of aftershave
on my shirt, man-perfume
surviving the laundry unforgotten.

The daughter of a famous ornithologist
lived down the street. Once, she opened

her father's shallow drawers for us:
hummingbirds, eyeless, row upon row,
uncountable, identical, with anklets of gold wire.
Like those tiny bodies—fusty, perfect,
labeled, dead—the children are mute now,
abandoned to dream of their fears
and amnesias as best they can.

My Lethe

A door blew open, and a black river
flowed into the house. It was my river,
invisible except to me. At night
it would come to me, and carry the flimsy raft
of my bed away with it, so I could feel
the current's preliminary cold caresses
throughout me, and hear its voice lapping
at the mind's peripheries, promising
it would carry me into the world
inside this one, and it would.
I spent most of my childhood there,
in the granite mountains of the north,
where I might meet Odysseus on the trail,
or a centaur groomed for town,
his hooves gilt. I drank my river's anesthesia,
but its immortal water goes on
gushing from a stone mouth,
saying what it knows all day, all night.
Like thunder it enters my body
without permission and stays
as long as it likes. If I submit
to its undertow, it lets me hold
a cold god almost in my arms.

Sideshows

A man sat the girl who was eventually
returned to her family unharmed
on a marble mantelpiece,
naked, very high and cold.
She sat first one way then other ways
while he looked. Sometimes he set up
bright umbrellas and she played
gypsy girl, cowgirl, little tomboy
with a girl's bathing suit on backward
splashing in a pool of moonlight.

The far-off but tremendous
battles of dinosaurs thunder through the ground—
the Whiplash, the Ferris wheel slowing back
down to the place where
the man rocked the car so hard
you had to hold on to the bar
so he could touch you.

Do you sometimes suffer
a stab of insight into another's sentience,
unwanted knowledge, unbidden,
both animal and human?
A dog lost a fight so his owner
doused him with gas and lit him.
The holes of our eyes met—I saw
the shriveled spirit that survived.
It ran off to join the circus of semen and murder.

The Dark Rides

The girl who likes to get high
wonders if her flower will ever unfurl,
or will there be a tight not-fully-formed
green part that chars before blooming?
Can something pinch an infant bud
so there's a missing branch forever?

Dark attractions was another
name for the dark rides:
the Gold Mine with candy wrappers
stapled to a fence for the loot,
the Black Swans "love tunnel,"
where couples whimpered
and squealed. In her underworld,
just below this one, not an inch away,
there's always a midway strung
with garish lights, and a small paddock
of saddled ponies circling nose to tail.

To explain her own childhood, she studies
the childhood of the girl who was eventually
returned to her family unharmed,
though her bad luck dates from that time,
as well as the illusion of looking through glass.
There are lessons she's learned and unlearned
ten thousand times, caught in the drag
of one pole or another, the need to know
the wordless truth of what she is,

and the equally fierce and endless denials,
the pure-hearted questions answered by lies,
the prayers subsumed by smoke or thinned
to nothing in the fumes of alcohol.
She longs to know whatever it is
she keeps herself from knowing. Or rather,
the knowledge comes to her but she loses it
again among the small herd of centaurs
she keeps on her desk, of which only one
is female—bronze, late nineteenth century,
grapevine crown, anatomy explicit (though tiny).
The horse's maneless neck becomes
the maiden's torso, the two bodies one.
You have to fuck the horse to fuck the girl.

Mask of a Maiden

My lips are clay, for centuries unkissed.
I thought middle age would not pass so quickly.
Time is cruel. I look in the mirror.
Now the word *cruel* scares me.

My ambition was once
to write the starlit poems of our age,
our final words, which in any case
are just graffiti from here on out,
yesteryear straight through to the afterlife
(though wasn't the middle part
supposed to be longer?).

I wanted words to contain consciousness,
so I was a child until I was old.

Cold Water

Whenever Grandma thought
I was pushing my luck, she'd say,
You're not skating on thin ice—
you're skating on cold water.

Sometimes instead of just washing the dishes,
I stick a plumber's snake of anger
down the drain, then stop myself.
It's a duet I play with myself.

Here comes the mosquito
for the third time.
The larvae we wondered about
were mosquito, of course!
In the end I do kill it.
One miss, and then I kill it.

Upstream, downstream—
where am I right now?
I don't even know
the river's name.

Poetry's absurd, like building
a birdcage out of birds.
Besides, since every thought was once
a beforethought, all words
are clouds in the mind's afterlife.

I'm a factory, very busy,
a manufacturer of poor quality
word-clouds. Why listen to me?

Snakeskin

When I lie on the floor with a dog
and half-capture her so I can brush her,
check her ears and eyes, her nose
and teeth and tongue, and slicken
her feathery pale belly with a cat brush,
I'm not sure where I've been when I come back.
Something goes and comes back.
Sentience, consciousness, soul, spirit—
for lack of better words I call it *mind*.
It has no name for itself.

When I was a young snake
and sloughed off my first skin,
reborn a quicksilver rivulet in the grass,
my body was a question answered
by the crisp gray lace it left behind.

Things do not come in and out of being
in words. There are no words until after.

Forensic Interludes

I'm drawn to the theaters of autopsy
and morgue, crime dramas like
night classes in biology and criminal psych.
I love the forensic interludes, the sixty-second
music-video collages of techno-lab experiments,
beakers of vivid liquids, medley of machine-voices
detecting lies and matching prints.
No words, just music and visuals.
And then the music changes;
the detectives are back with fresh
kill. Evidently, they need proof
that even a kiss disintegrates,
as, evidently, do I, though
I already know what's at the dead
center of everything: it's a little squelt of shit.

Look at my handwriting: script
hardening like the grapevines
scrawled on the shed, handwriting
very like my father's, which got smaller
and smaller until the name and address
he wrote on an envelope were
no bigger than the stamp.

When arthritis bites at my hands,
I say to myself, *This is how it will be someday.*
This is how it is now.
A thought begins to form but I miscarry it.

This happens with increasing frequency,
probably just the synapses sparking and going out,
or a dearth of neurotransmitters,
but it makes me wonder what it is
that's watching itself die.

War Porn

I failed to write a poem about what the famous
quarterback and his friends did to those dogs
in the Bad Newz Kennels. How they beat
and starved them, then sent them psychotic
into death-fights. Unpromising dogs:
drowned, hanged, electrocuted, set on fire.
Set on fire, electrocuted, hanged, drowned.
What buys the right to drown a dog?
And that's where I'd get stuck.
I couldn't answer. I couldn't even
fully form the question.

Negligent Worldicide

The bear climbed over the mountain,
and what do you think he saw?
History raging and ravaging, carving up
the one and only body of the earth,
the new century already broken-into,
ransacked, roads unsafe,
infants crawling on the landfill.

We should speak only of urgent things.
The earth was heaven once, and now it's hell.
Since it's already begun to embalm itself,
let's assume that these are close to
our last words. That's what I mean by urgent.

Oh fuck, I'm going to have to take it
in my arms again. I'm going to have to
love it again, dear corpse of earth,
dear tough-muscled body of river
still ignorant of putrefaction,
of the slow downstream parade
of dead beings. I say goodbye
to petals every day. Lilac, wild rose,
poppy disintegrating, one moment
a flower and the next no flower.

The Fifth Precept

Do not cloud the mind, says the Fifth Precept.
My mind has clouds of its own,
hypomanic storms, wild flights!
Let's not be squeamish or coy;
it's only biochemistry.
Hypomania's a fuel; I run on it
(and psychopharmacology).

Thunderstorms elate me; my mind
draws a charge from the sky,
but there's no letdown, just
heightened attention gradually subsiding.
*Sometimes ideas run through my head so that
I cannot sleep. I'm inclined to rush from one activity
to another without pausing for enough rest.
I am sometimes more talkative than usual
or feel a pressure to keep talking.
Sooner or later I wear myself out.**

I asked a teacher how a cloud should sit.
He said, *Sit among clouds.*
Zazen, what ridiculous and arduous work,
following the homeless dog home!
Sometimes I sit instead on the banks

*Bipolar II characteristics (in italic) have been lifted from the *Diagnostic and Statistical Manual of Mental Disorders* (*DSM-IV-TR*, American Psychiatric Association, 2000). The list is partial and rearranged, but otherwise verbatim.

of the Forensic River, television, and watch
them unzip the shroud of the exhumed child.
Sometimes I study the monkey-antics of mind,
or wonder what opium would be like.
I feel like *Voyager*, the spacecraft sent out
by Jimmy Carter with an intergalactic greeting
from Earth, and a map of how to find me.

Sayonara Marijuana Mon Amour

In the mornings black tea uplifts me,
and at night I invite wine to tell
its stories in my mouth. If I nap,
a different mind awakes than the one
that lay down and dreamed of swimming.
Both dreaming and swimming alter consciousness.
So do zazen, weeding, and sex.
Marijuana makes me self-
and unself-conscious simultaneously,
like playing with dogs.

The first time I got high, we gathered
at the monument in East Rock Park.
I read the plaque to the Union Dead.
Moving from one mind to another
was familiar to me, as was the sensation
of watching myself, as if the dead and I
were the audience, and my friends
were real, and in the world.
As a kid I believed that the dead
lay inside the monuments,
that each monument was a tomb,
proof of death one old stone wall away,
the same distance as the friends.

Whatever it is in me that was born striving
was also born craving and clinging.
Once, when I'd drunk too much wine,

the dogs and I stood in the snowy yard,
their wet black nostrils working,
drawing in scents from a realm
unknown to me. I looked up at the great
dust-light of stars, and there was my question
spelled out for me, in plain sight.
But *whose* question was it?

I must not want to be fully enlightened,
since I do not devote myself entirely to it.
I like distraction. Whenever I'm distracted,
a new room appears for my perusal,
or an ocean, or a neighborhood lit
by childhood's untrustworthy flashlights,
half dreamed-up, half memory.
Or lit by the alpenglow or northern lights,
under the constellation Not Here Not Now,
where I have wasted most of my life.

I often berate myself, renew my vows,
forsake all toys, recite the Gatha of Atonement.
I pledge austerity; I scorn squander.
No (imaginary teacher talking), *that misses it.*
Toys are neither right nor wrong.

When I wonder which of these nights
will be the night I renounce it,
the spank in the intake surprises me again,
and I return its resinous kiss.
It tastes of every mouth that ever

stopped kissing me to ask me
what consciousness was (very few,
but those are the ones I remember).

Playgrounds of Being

Awake at three, snow falling in the dark,
I breathe cold air in, warm air out.

Insomnia sounds like someone twiddling
the radio dial: interspliced commercials,
Mahler, rock and roll, female and male
persuasion, argument and song.
Ha-ha! Here I am in a delicate hush
listening instead to the stations
of the self, the substanceless sounds
of my own being obliterating the world.

And what if tonight is the last night,
the grand finale, the nevermore?
I lie here wondering if the yearning
to be awake is a yearning to disappear.
Sometimes I'm afraid of the ever-flowing
river of the work, afraid that to ask
a single question forever is to be a stone.

One of the dogs yips and sighs in sleep,
then settles into breathing that makes
the sound of a hammock longing,
longing, the soft complaints
of wood to rope, rope to wood.
Why can't the mind bear to stay
in the beauties that surround it?

Over and over I lose myself,
invent myself again. I must be
a multitude of lost inventors.

Inside me, the snows of sleep
begin to drift, erasing my footprints
and the paw prints of the dogs.
The little engine of thinking sputters
and dies in the great silence.

Some people will say that these words
make a dull clopping. I hope they sound
like horses on the road—plainspoken.

Clouds and Water

Before there was a bowl of water,
before the backhoe forever changed
the wetland darkness of the place,
I'd watch the pink and charcoal cirrus
come in and out of being in a sky
that was solitary, not yet
reflected back to itself.

I have no words for the junco
lighting on my hand
as I lift down the empty feeder,
or for the tracks around
the always-running spring,
my own comings and goings.
When I go, wherever I go,
I don't know it, but I know it
afterward, when I come back.

I thought zazen was a splitter,
a maul. Wrong. And it's not a river,
an eraser, or an exercise.
It isn't even tall grass lying down
in wind, practicing to be tall grass.

Sorry, these words are just
the sound of shovel hitting ledge.
Who wouldn't rather listen
to the ins and outs of wind,

the freezing and thawing of water
descending the stone ladder of the spillway,
or watch the quiet cities of the clouds?

Whether slumming in the ghost-lands
of memory or striving for the pure precincts
that lie before thinking, I chase an animal
I rarely see, though clearly it frequents the pond.
Sometimes when I kneel to drink where it drank,
its face looks back at me.

Tenderfoot

I ride the chute and swim
out into the dark panes of cold,
then climb the glacial stairs to lie on hot granite,
the same slabs on which my young father
screwed his girlfriends sixty-something years ago.

The locals call it Tenderfoot,
one of the deep pools, miles upstream;
you rarely see a stranger there.
The lure and the dare is a steep sluice
of water through bedrock—
thirty feet in too-late-to-stop mind
then a shock of froth that flips
you backward once or twice
before it lets you go. There's a rare blue
iridescence in the rocks, labradorite,
which goes gray when dry,
but underwater is a trove of jewels.

How easily mind swims into silence:
a faraway floor of stones wavering in sun,
clouds of bubbles spilled by falls,
no sign of human life. No words.

How Zen Ruins Poets

Before I knew that mind
could never marry the words
it loved, in which it lost itself,
in which it dressed itself,
in which it sang its most secret
tender and bitter hymns,
I also loved the thrill of thinking.
Since birth I've swum in the clear,
decisive muscles of its currents,
the places where the water seemed
to reconsider its course before continuing,
then the sudden onrush of falls.
I lived inside language, its many musics,
its rough, lichen-crusted stones,
its hemlocks bowed in snow.
Words were my altar and my school.
Wherever they took me, I went,
and they came to me, winged and bearing
the beautiful twigs and litter
of life's meaning, the songs of truth.

Then a question arose in me:
What language does the mind
speak before thinking, before
thinking gives birth to words?
I tried to write without embellishment,
to tell no lies while keeping death in mind.
To write what was still unthought-about.

Stripped to their thinnest selves,
words turn transparent, to windows
through which I sometimes glimpse
what's just beyond them.
There, a tiny flash—did you see it?
There it is again!

Good-bad Zazen

Why would anyone want to sit
cross-legged for an hour a day,
motionless, every itch unscratched,
striving for clear mind, fighting sleep?
Right now I'm part human, part dog,
part hungry ghost, part bodhisattva,
longing for the afternoon I'm already in.

Around me the whole dark immediate
forest is collapsing, the pines purple
with storm-light, the house suddenly still.
I killed two baby trout today.
I was fishing the brook barbless,
after little ones for the pond.
These two swallowed the hook.
Brookies: five inches, four inches.
Now I atone for it all.

For years I sat zazen intermittently
while reading fervently, a form of bullshit.
I wore a cloak of asceticism, and wandered
from abandoned outpost to abandoned outpost,
reading each wind-toughened note
on the front doors:
The livestock wandered off to who-knows-where.

Sometimes I still go swimming secretly
in the joyful garrulous river,

the delicious white-water of thought,
or play on the ladders of logic,
re-asking Dogen's question:
If we're all born Buddhas,
why seek enlightenment?
The dogs know. Look at them,
wrestling the ancient eternal questions,
play-crouching, mock-fighting over a stick.

How I feel age coming on me now,
fast, suddenly way too fast,
tremor in my hands typing this,
playing the keyboard like a piano,
puppet bones dancing, clickety-click.
My very bones, right here in front of me!
It's a matter of life and death.

The Fork

A wooden Buddha gazes down
upon my desk from a small shelf
painted the same color as the walls:
Chinese Dragon. Beside him,
a picture Lucy drew when she was six
shows a bird with human face
and the words *Have fun being a parrot*
written below it in parrot colors.

Earnestly I vow to become one,
sleek-feathered, able to fly pathless
above human traffic in a kingdom
of light and air, no suffering.
I can't go on feigning surprise
at the kalpas it's taken so far,
since they're all my kalpas.

I follow the path, but it forks.
To the right, faint blazes hardly ruckle the bark.
The trail follows the brook all the way to Nirvana,
where I have never been. To the left,
the path soon splits again: right to Nirvana,
left to the trail that forks.

Old-lady Cautious on the Stairs

I keep my hand on the banister,
take one step at a time,
pause at the window.

Petals in the air!
No, still winter.

I look out across the whitening mountains.
My dog is squatting
right in the middle of the driveway.

From a Distance

Of all the selves I've invented,
the ones most fixed in memory
are the horse-child startling,
the dog-child sniffing the still-warm ashes
where the smell of food has almost been erased.
Child-mammals, clothed in dead leaves
that slip right off their shivering,
still haunting the snowy woods of dreams,
the twilit smoke of past and future lives...
Not ghosts, although they vanish and reappear.
Not human, for they were never born.
And all the others, their successors,
where have they gone, my forebears,
my lineage? And where am I now,
bereft of their company? Death will come
and take me to them, and a new self will begin
to ask these questions as if for the first time.

Zazen and Opium

I know what I have to give up.
It's not the flashy green commotion
of leaves this August evening,
garden blackening, drinking,
or the dogs unsettled by thunder
I can't yet hear. It's not the teakettle's
ongoing quarrel with itself,
or the snow's beauty coming from far away
to cover the beauty now ascending.

There's no sense giving up
what will be taken from me anyway,
first youth, now middle age departing,
the eastern woodlands stricken
by acid and blight,
beloved sky blue-blackening,
cedar waxwings swooping
low over the pond, feeding,
fattening for their voyage
to a world devoid of us.

I know what I need to know.
No path lies ahead of me.
Where I go, it follows.
I lead it to the monastery,
where I sit steadfast in the very early hours,
a pure Zen Yankee candle, my flame a vow
to save all sentient beings, beginning with myself.

I also take it into the vast playgrounds
of distraction, confusion, intoxication, desire,
drugged by anxiety and second guesses,
and deep into television's alternative wilderness.
What a beautiful war I wage,
the two poles equal magnets,
perfectly matched, married—
my own perfect paralysis.

Present then absent then present,
I inhabit the moment or do not.
It's one continuous decision.
The waxwings don't decide which insects
to eat tonight, nor wind pause to think before
clouding the mirror of the trees.
They leave no monuments.
Me, I'm always forsaking one place for another,
breaking branches to mark my way home,
taking leave of the tall grasses
heavy with seed-heads I crush underfoot,
birches vivid in storm-light, dogs just groomed,
fearful of thunder under the desk.
I smell garlic. Russell is making a marinade
for the trout he'll grill beneath an umbrella.
I realize, then forget, then realize that mind
is an ax that splits the one continuous moment.
Lightning! Scared dogs! Dinner! Brook music!
My eye goes home to the pond,
the bluestone slates I laid in the low places,
rain-shining their way to the water.

About the Author

Chase Twichell is the author of six previous books of poetry, most recently *Dog Language* (Copper Canyon Press). She is also the co-translator, with Tony K. Stewart, of *The Lover of God*, poems by Rabindranath Tagore (Copper Canyon), and co-editor, with Robin Behn, of *The Practice of Poetry: Writing Exercises from Poets Who Teach* (HarperCollins). Twichell's work has been awarded grants from the National Endowment for the Arts, the John Simon Guggenheim Memorial Foundation, and the Artists Foundation. She's the recipient of an Award in Literature from the American Academy of Arts and Letters, the Alice Fay Di Castagnola Award from the Poetry Society of America, and the Hugh Ogden Poetry Prize from Trinity College. From 1999 to 2009 she was the editor of Ausable Press. She lives in the Adirondacks with her husband, the novelist Russell Banks.

The Chinese character for poetry is made up of two parts: "word" and "temple." It also serves as pressmark for Copper Canyon Press.

Since 1972, Copper Canyon Press has fostered the work of emerging, established, and world-renowned poets for an expanding audience. The Press thrives with the generous patronage of readers, writers, booksellers, librarians, teachers, students, and funders — everyone who shares the belief that poetry is vital to language and living.

Major funding has been provided by:

Amazon.com

Anonymous

Beroz Ferrell & The Point, LLC

Golden Lasso, LLC

Lannan Foundation

National Endowment for the Arts

Cynthia Lovelace Sears and Frank Buxton

Washington State Arts Commission

For information and catalogs:

COPPER CANYON PRESS
Post Office Box 271
Port Townsend, Washington 98368
360-385-4925
www.coppercanyonpress.org

NATIONAL
ENDOWMENT
FOR THE ARTS

WASHINGTON STATE
ARTS COMMISSION

This book is set in two contemporary transitional typefaces. The text is set in Whitman, developed from Kent Lew's studies of W.A. Dwiggins's Caledonia. The heads are set in Mrs Eaves, designed by Zuzana Licko from her studies of Baskerville. Book design and composition by Valerie Brewster, Scribe Typography. Printed on archival-quality paper at McNaughton & Gunn, Inc.